Bruce Fogle was born in Toronto and studied
veterinary medicine at the Ontario Veterinary
College. After coming to London on a
post-graduate travel scholarship, he worked as
an assistant and then in his own small animal
practice and it was this experience that kindled
his interest in the roles pets play in their owner's
lives. He is a founder member of the Society for
Companion Animal Studies and, in 1980,
organised the first international scientific
symposium on the human-companion animal
bond. Dr Fogle is the editor of the text book
Interrelations Between People and Pets and has
been a guest speaker at scientific meetings and
universities in Britain, Europe and America. His
contact comfort needs are met by his three
children, his Golden Retriever and his wife, the
actress Julia Foster.

Pets and their People

BRUCE FOGLE

Illustrations by LALLA WARD

SPHERE BOOKS LIMITED

First published in Great Britain by
William Collins & Sons Ltd 1983
Copyright © in the text Bruce Fogle 1983
Copyright © in the illustrations Lalla Ward 1983
Published by Sphere Books Ltd 1986
27 Wrights Lane, London W8 5TZ
Reprinted 1986

TRADE
MARK

Printed and bound in Great Britain by
Cox & Wyman Ltd, Reading

Contents

Acknowledgements

The episodes that I recount in this book are from my personal experience but the interpretations I put on them are based on the ideas of many others. I thank them all for their ideas and apologize if I have misinterpreted any of them.

My interest in the relationships between people and their pets, and specifically in who is doing what and to whom, was stimulated by encounters early in my practice career. I am grateful to all my patients and their owners for giving me the experience and the opportunity to write about them.

Gail Cornish unravelled my longhand and produced a legible manuscript and Maxine Clark made sure that my practice functioned smoothly when I was away at meetings or symposia. I appreciate what they both did.

Finally, I'd like to thank my wife for introducing me to her dog. Honey, our Golden Retriever is still around, although very old now. During the past twelve years, I have learned more about canine behaviour and about human behaviour from her than from anyone or anything else. I am grateful to her for just being there.

Dedication

Carol Ann Brant, a descendant of Chief Joseph Brant of the Mohawk nation, was asked to speak at an international conference on wilderness conservation. In her presentation, she read from a letter from Chief Seathl of the Duwamish Tribe, in what is now the State of Washington. Chief Seathl was being asked to sign a treaty to sell his tribe's land to the American Government and to move to a reservation. In 1855 he wrote to the President of the United States:

"If I decide to accept I will make one condition. The white man must treat the beasts of this land as his brothers. What is man without the beasts? If all the beasts were gone, man would die from great loneliness of spirit, for whatever happens to the beasts also happens to the man. All things are connected. Whatever befalls the earth befalls the sons of the earth."

This book is dedicated to him. It is also dedicated to his spiritual successor, one of the next generation's settlers in Washington State, Leo Bustad.

Leo Bustad is an anomaly. He is one of the funniest men I have ever met, and one of the most serious. He is Professor and Dean at the School of Veterinary Medicine at Washington State University; a man who has spent his professional life as a hard scientist in a hard science. And he is one of the softest people I have met. He is a man with zest and unmitigated enthusiasm, who has uplifted many more people than me alone. He has scientific training to back him up, but he thinks as did Chief Seathl. The two men are of a rare and valuable kind.

Prologue

Let me tell you about yesterday. It was a slightly busier than normal Tuesday. The day started with a few straightforward appointments. Kizzy Warren, an eighteen-year-old cat, was the first patient, and she was brought in simply for a blood sample to be taken to monitor her kidney condition. Kizzy is not as agile as she was. Once, when I went on a house visit to see her, I was surprised at the number of cushions lying on the floor around the furniture. Mrs Warren explained that they were actually strategically placed. Kizzy still liked walking on the arms of chairs but her balance wasn't what it used to be. The cushions were placed to break her fall.

Jason Benedict, a slightly aggressive black Pug, was next. He was in for his yearly booster vaccination and a general health check. Mr Benedict enjoys watching horse jumping on television. When horses are on television, Jason must, however, be locked in another room. Jason hates horses with a passion, and if he sees one on TV, he barks and attacks.

Jason was followed by Heidi Summers, a Pyrenean Mountain Dog suffering from a hind leg partial paralysis as a result of a wire injury to the groin. Mrs Summers had been in tears when the injury occurred because she quite rightly understood that, although a small dog can get by on three legs, a dog as big as a Pyrenean needs all four working most of the time in order to enjoy a decent life. Heidi was improving and the prognosis was very good. A health certificate for a Persian kitten going to Saudi Arabia was next, then a first vaccination for an eight-week-old pup belonging to a young couple living up the road. A regular visitor, Mrs Kaplan, was next with her budgie. She brought it in to have its beak trimmed, but I explained to her, as I had several times before, that it was quite unnecessary, so she told me instead about her problems with her neighbour. Mrs Kaplan was followed by Captain Morgan with his Gordon Setter Amber. Amber had made several serious attacks on other dogs and had been made to wear a muzzle. He was a handsome dog, benign with people but ferocious with other dogs. The Morgans had been in before to discuss his aggressiveness, and although they felt too self-conscious to contact an animal behaviourist, they had changed their routines so that the dog was exercised at different times of the day and didn't meet his "enemies". Captain Morgan's son had forgotten to put the muzzle on the previous evening and Amber had attacked a neighbour's poodle. The family had decided that the risk was too great; that a child might be injured in the future, and had brought Amber in to be put down. We had already discussed the alternatives exhaustively and dismissed them all so, with pain to the owners and to me, but with none to the dog, I carried out their request.

The morning continued with similar cases. I patched up the savaged poodle, spayed a cat, castrated another, removed a growth from inside the mouth of an English Setter, who is so allergic to grass, and so untreatable, that the owners can only exercise her on sand, earth or concrete; and removed a skin tumour from a standard poodle.

Once the morning's cases were through, I had two lunch-time house visits. The first was to Miss Patch, a woman on supplementary benefit who spends most of her income on feeding the feral cats of Maida Vale. One of these cats had an ear infection and, after getting suitably lacerated trying to catch it, I treated the ear and let the cat explode out of the window. The next visit was happier (and financially more rewarding – how can you charge someone on supplementary benefit?). It was to visit Tara, a Cairn Terrirer who had produced four pups the previous day. Having seen that all was well, I returned to the Clinic where I found not lunch but a personal friend waiting there with his ten-year-old Old English Sheepdog. Both looked anxious and forlorn. The dog had suddenly lost all its energy. A feel of the belly, and the history, suggested a bleeding tumour in the spleen and the nurses prepared for immediate surgery. While the owner sat on the stairs outside the operating room, and his wife, children and nanny fretted upstairs with my wife, Oliver, the dog, was given his various intravenous fluids and drugs and the tumour and spleen were removed. Oliver's owner runs a business from a building called Oliver House. Do you think he loves his dog?

The afternoon appointments followed the routine of the morning. Some good dogs and cats, and some not so good dogs and cats, and some good owners and some not so good owners. At six o'clock we got an alarm call from the owner of Tara, the Cairn Terrier. Tara had taken one of the pups out of the house into the garden and down a rabbit hole. She had been spending a considerable amount of time down this hole before she whelped, and now it was obvious why. I told the owner to lock her in if she came back, and when she cockily returned to get the next pup, the owners prevented her from carrying out her plan to move her litter into a more natural and safer environment. The pup left in the rabbit's nest was gently dug out and returned to the litter. A blanket was placed over the window, the cardboard "nest" was put under a table and the door to the room in which she was staying was shut. Tara's behaviour was perfectly normal for a dog. It was only the owners and their veterinarian who found it unacceptable.

The mini-crisis with Tara had delayed my final obligation of the day. Five years ago, when she was seven years old, Sally Winterbottom had her first and only litter of pups, at the Clinic. Sally, a Yellow Labrador, had my own dog's personality; soft, gentle, with perhaps a mite too much gloom and doom, but she had great ease of character and her reliability was such that, while she was with us for that week, she would come upstairs to ask to be let out, would wander outside to squat in the gutter, and then come straight back in to nurse her pups. Perhaps it was her instinctive mothering ability; perhaps it was her name (after all Sally and Hubert Winterbottom are two Labradors' names that are not easily forgotten); perhaps it was the dogs' relationship with and significance for the owners; but for whatever reason, I had promised that when the time came I would euthanize Sally in her own home. There was nothing unusual in that, other than that Sally lived one and a half hours from London.

I didn't mind the drive but, as always, hated the reason for it. Sally had developed malignant mammary tumours, and although we had postponed the decision, the reality of the situation had to be faced last night. She woofed a "hello" and then followed me into the lounge, wagging her tail. With Mr Winterbottom talking to me and to her, I asked her to lie down and give me her paw. She did. I gave her the barbiturate in the vein in her leg and she died. Because she was so big, I helped the gardener bury her. At least there was something gratifying in stomping the earth down on her grave and replacing the turf. I felt happier, even contented, to have participated in that final act. I drove slowly back to London, taking the old road rather than the motorway. Oliver was recovering from his surgery marvellously. His owners had telephoned to ask how he was, but the number I had for them was an old one and their telephone was ex-directory. While I made myself a sandwich, my wife popped over to their house to tell them all was well.

It was a typical day, prolonged by the drive into the country in the evening. I did what all veterinarians who treat small animals do every day. I treated pets preventatively or in emergency for physical injuries and disease. I had a good training at university to do these things. I also killed two animals. I wasn't trained in how to decide when to kill a pet, only in how to do it. I met a lady who totally neglects herself in order to spend all of her time and money on stray cats. I was never told about these people; about why they feel the overwhelming need to care for animals but in doing so disregard themselves. I listened to Mrs Kaplan tell me about her neighbours. Before I qualified I had thought that I would be spending my time treating diseased and injured animals. I didn't know that Mrs Kaplan would use her budgie as a good excuse to tell me about her problems.

In my first ten years in practice it soon became evident that the relationships people have with their pets, and the responsibilities of their veterinarians, are far more intricate and complicated than they outwardly seem. But when I tried to find out more about the relationship between people and pets, I drew a blank. In searching for some of the answers I chanced upon a lot of fascinating people and a number of even more fascinating facts. The chapters that follow are the result of some of those encounters.

CHAPTER ONE

Why pets?

Attachments between people and pets are viewed with about the same scientific interest as are soap operas and Barry Manilow's voice. All of these ooze sentimentality, and in our culture sentiment is not thought worthy of serious scientific examination. A pet owner's relationship with his or her pet only becomes important to the medical or scientific community if it transpires that the person is also a chainsaw killer or a foot fetishist.

But pet ownership has been in existence for at least 30,000 years, and probably much longer. In the English-speaking world it is the normal practice. Over half of all households in Britain and North America keep pets. Clearly pet ownership is an institution of importance both to pets and to people, otherwise it would not have lasted so long, nor would it be so widespread today. What are the benefits of the relationship, and why did we choose to have pets in the first place.

Although we would like to think that we are unique, the human animal, like all other creatures, is the product of the genes carried in its cells and passed on from generation to generation. Our genetic programming is the same now as it was when we roamed the earth's forests and plains hunting and gathering for a living. Thinking back, then, to the time when animals were first domesticated is not an abstract exercise. Our basic physiological processes were the same then as they are now. We loved. We hated. We felt parental. We liked to touch warm, soft things. We needed security. We wanted to feel important. We wanted to be loved. We needed to talk. We liked to laugh.

All these urges developed to help us survive as a pre-agricultural species, fitting into our own niche in the balance of life. So where do pets come in?

There are two basic theories concerning why people first chose to have pets. One is that they were domesticated to serve some useful and utilitarian purpose in the environment of the time and that they subsequently became companions. The other is simply the reverse: that animals became companions first and only later were they used, and specifically bred, to serve the practical needs of their owners.

The first argument, domestication for a specific purpose, contains a number of interesting hypotheses. It has been suggested for example that the domestication of dogs may have begun with captured young wolves who were destined for the dinner table. Some might have escaped this fate, been tamed and then bred from selectively for docility.

I must admit that there are some patients I am obliged to see whom I would rather see on a dinner table than on the examination table. But the practicality of Chihuahua Cordon Bleu is the same now as it was then. Carnivores such as dogs and cats are simply not efficient meat producers. They must eat too much meat themselves if they are to "flesh out" and be suitable for consumption. Dog was, and still is, eaten in various parts of the world, notably in the Far East and in Central and Southern America, but it is likely that the custom developed as a temporary starvation measure rather than through planned breeding for the purpose. Cat, apparently was not, and still is not, on human menus.

Another hypothesis is that the domestication of dogs and cats arose from a parasitic relationship, in which humans took advantage of the superior hunting skills of wolves and wild cats. Human hunting parties, it is suggested, would follow wolf packs to the prey, allow them to capture it, and then deprive them of it.

Right up to the present day, however, hunting dogs have all had to be modified in the same way and for the same reason – so that we can keep up with them either on foot or on horseback. It would have been impossible to keep up with the wolf pack, and it seems unlikely that this relationship could have been a cause for domestication. The same can be

said of a similar suggestion, that our ancestors exploited the fact that dogs protect their territory by barking to gain added protection for themselves. Dogs, however, have been selectively bred to bark; wolves bark far less than any breed of dog so the relationship can hardly have begun for this reason.

There is much more to recommend the alternative theory – that animals were domesticated as pets and only later were used for specific purposes. Ancient attitudes towards pets, for example, suggest strongly that the original relationship between pets and people was one of companionship. Dogs were venerated in Egypt and this veneration had a basis in survival. The very life of the Egyptians depended on the annual overflowing of the Nile which was announced by the appearance of a certain star, Sirius. When Sirius rose above the horizon, flocks were removed to higher ground, as were families. The star was their guard and protector. Its fidelity earned it the name "dog star", and it was worshipped. But if the Egyptians thought that there was nothing that showed more fidelity than a dog, it is obvious that dogs had already been companions of people for a considerable time.

Not all cultures regarded pets highly, it is true. In Islamic countries contact with a dog, especially with its saliva, must be followed by a ritual cleansing and purification because the dog is possessed by a "wicked and malignant spirit". Well, in most Islamic countries dogs certainly are prone to a wicked and malignant spirit. It is called rabies. The Bible, like the Koran, also speaks of dogs with abhorrence but this was because part of Jewish Law was designated to preserve the Israelites from idolatry. The dog was one of their neighbours idols. As the Egyptians venerated, so the Israelites despised.

Even religious strictures may be insufficient to prevent the development of companionship between people and pets. I remember, shortly after graduating, having a dog that had been in a road traffic accident brought to me. The dog was dead on arrival, although still quivering. I told the owner that nothing could be done, that death had been almost instantaneous. He gently put his hand on his dog's chest, burying his fingers in the fur, and quietly, almost inaudibly, recited the "Shema", the Jewish prayer reaffirming one's faith in God.

The theory that animals were originally domesticated as pets also has a common sense ring to it. Every week someone brings me a sick baby mouse, sparrow, pigeon, or even rat, that they have found. My classmates in Canada are brought baby racoons, skunks, foxes and wolves as well. Why? Why do so many of us go out of our way, and incur expense, to help orphaned or injured animals? And what do we do with the animals once they are successfully treated?

We do it, naturally, because we don't like to see suffering. But we do it for other reasons as well. Anyone who has seen week-old kittens or pups knows what I mean. You want to touch them. You want to cuddle them. You want to feed them. You want to play with them. You want to care for them. Bearing in mind that, genetically, our ancestors of 50,000 years ago resembled us very closely, is there any reason to suspect that they would not have acted in a similar fashion?

Once you stroke, fondle, cuddle, feed, play with and care for something, you're hooked. We are programmed to be hooked. Part of the reason we first chose to have pets is biological and out of our control. But why did pets first choose to have people?

*And what do we do
with the animals once
they are treated?*

There are two species that have been so oustandingly successful in their partnership with the human animal that they have
effectively eliminated all other contenders; they are, of
course, the dog and the cat.

At the time when pets first accepted life in the company of
humans, the human animal lived in small communities of
closely related individuals who were interdependent upon
one another as hunter/gatherers. They were, of course,
sociable, as we are today, and communal in their living
habits. Each community had its home range or territory for
hunting and gathering, and it is assumed that these territories
were protected by the community from any incursions by
strangers. It is also assumed that within each community
there was a dominance/subordinance relationship between
the leader and the followers. Leadership was based on
physical strength and mental acuity.

Now look at a typical wolf pack. The pack is a social group
of ten to twenty genetically related individuals in a strict
dominance/subordinance relationship. It lives communally,
hunting on its home territory and excluding all strange
wolves. The leader of the pack is the leader because of
physical strength and intelligence.

Cats, too, are far more sociable than was at one time thought. They are highly territorial and, though more independent than dogs, show dominance/subordinance relationships. The major difference between cat colonies and dog packs is that a "typical" cat colony has one tom cat who covers a large territory and several females, each with a territory, within his territory.

Dogs and cats have developed social organizations involving methods of communication, territory and play. So has the human. The human colony, because of the social structure it had, offered the dog and the cat a social structure similar to the ones they had evolved themselves. In other words, both dogs and cats were preadapted, and preadapted better than almost any other living things, to living symbiotically or in harmony with the human. Some of these preadaptations are fascinating.

Take play, for example. Play, in both childhood and adulthood, is important to us. It is good for survival. Through play, we practice and perfect the skills we need in life. Darwin said that play was usually connected with laughter and fun; that pleasure and enjoyment are essential to it.

Of all animals, the dog shows more play activity as an adult than any other species of animal. Farley Mowat's dog, Mutt, used to hunt crayfish and frogs. In Mowat's book *The Dog Who Wouldn't Be*, he described Mutt's play activity this way.

"If crayfish were not abundant, or if the cove happened to be marshy, Mutt would hunt frogs instead. He did this purely for fun, since he never ate the frogs he caught. Nor would he catch a frog while it was on dry land. The trick was to chivy it into, and under, the water and try to locate it as it huddled on the bottom. Then Mutt's head would dart down with a speed and precision equal to that of his chief competitor, the great blue heron; and generally he would emerge with the frog held gently in his jaws. He would carry it to land, release it, and then chase it back into the water for another round."

Artificial selection has made Mutt play with frogs, but the dog's basic stock, the wolf, also plays as an adult. Adult cats do as well. So do adult humans. Might it be that the impulse to play was associated with the development of the relationship between people and pets?

It is now widely accepted that the human animal needs an optimal amount of stimulation to work "properly". In the presence of boredom, play can provide that stimulation. Play with animals is as stimulating as any other play.

Animals play best after they have been released from confinement, and captive animals play more than wild animals. There was once a bear at Basle Zoo in Switzerland who, during a pause in training, hopped on his scooter and did a few quick circuits, apparently for its own sake. Another bear, at the Berne Zoo, a bear who had no playthings, used to make snowballs.

Playing with an animal increases the chance of contact with it, and contact is important in the development of attachments or bonds. But you can only play with an animal if it wants to play with you. Why do dogs and cats let us do so?

Dogs and cats go through a relatively long and late socialization compared to other species. Ungulates, for example, are socialized with their species within hours of birth. Dogs and wolves, however, begin to develop broad social attachments only when they begin to explore, when their eyes open at about three weeks of age. This begins the sensitive period in the pup's development. If it is exposed to two different species at that time it will socialize to both. If, for example, a wolf pup is raised by humans from three

weeks of age, and it has no contact with wolves, it will only socialize with humans and will be unable to live successfully with wolves. If, however, it is removed from its mother at six to eight weeks, it has had time to socialize, to get to know its own species but is still capable of developing a bond or relationship with humans. This animal might show its primary allegiance to man, but it will still be able to mate successfully with its species. In other words, it is easy to tame. The tendency of socialized wolves to acknowledge the dominant status of humans is a pack characteristic of primary importance to the success of the relationship.

This prolonged socializing period means that dogs and cats can, during these weeks, attach themselves to us. Of all the species of canine, the wolf is the most highly social and was consequently the primary contender for domestication.

Max Eastman said "Dogs laugh, but they laugh with their tails." Well, we think they do. Dogs and cats are poor at vocal communication but their body postures and facial expressions are highly expressive. Some scientists feel that primates including the human, and canines including the dog, share similar facial expressions and that these are commonly used. If that is the case, it would be an argument for why pets chose us. If it is not, it is still important because we interpret the facial expressions of both in the same way. In veterinary medicine, unlike human medicine, there are no symptoms, only clinical signs. A dog might have an aversion to bright light. That is a clinical sign. Its brow might be furrowed. That is a clinical sign. Its eyes might be partly closed. That is a clinical sign. But it doesn't have a headache because that is a symptom. I would need the dog to tell me it had a headache. Nevertheless, I interpret the dog's facial expressions to mean that the Rank Organization's hammer is active in its head.

I have some advantages over my colleagues in human medicine. I can also observe the position of my patient's ears and tail. In fact, I don't see how medical doctors can make a diagnosis without them. Dogs and cats probably have a greater repertoire of visual social signals than most other non-primates. They communicate with facial expression, ear position, body posture, tail movement and the direction of gaze. When I vaccinate my Golden Retriever and she gazes off into the middle distance my wife interprets the gaze as stoicism. Unfortunately, I know it means "I'm subservient and wish to avoid a confrontation".

The human, the dog and the cat all have need of large repertoires of communication because all live in organized societies. Of all the canines, the wolf has the best range and, once again, this is probably why it was chosen for, and accepted, domestication.

Other than primates, dogs and cats are among the most intelligent land-living mammals. My mother might think that her budgie is brilliant, but budgies have not gone through evolutionary development as pack animals. Almost every day someone will tell me how clever their dog or cat is. Owners take great pride in their pets' intelligence. Well, why then didn't we choose primates for pets?

Primates have the ability to learn faster and to do more. But in fact their social habits, sanitary habits and very intelligence preclude them from ever being good pets. First of all, monkeys have terrible toilet habits – terrible to us, that is. But if you evolved as a tree-swinging creature, you probably wouldn't mind where you did your business either. Dogs, and more so cats, are fussy about their toilet habits. Carnivores are basically tidy. They are selective and predictable. Because they are ground living rather than tree living, their droppings can be a signal to predators of their presence, or the very opposite; they can be used to mark a territory. Monkeys, however, are almost impossible to house train.

Monkeys are also aggressive in a competitive way. Because of this they are dangerous and unpredictable. I once had regularly to lance abscesses to the fingers of a diabetic African Green monkey, who would not counter insulin injections from its owner. Sometimes it would meekly give me its hand, as if it knew that the lancing and cleansing made it feel better. Yet at other times there would be fire in his eyes, true venom, and he would shriek and spit and try his utmost to attack my face.

Probably one of the major reasons we did not choose monkeys as pets is because they demand so much attention. Cats and dogs require attention as well, but not as much as monkeys. Beware of the frustrated monkey! It can be overwhelmingly destructive and genuinely spiteful. Attempts have been made in recent years to harness the monkey's need for activity, for the benefit of people. Capuchin monkeys, an easy-going species as monkeys go, have been trained to assist a house-bound man, paralysed from the neck down, by feeding him, picking up his mouth stick if he drops it, answering the door and doing odd jobs. The researchers, the animal behaviourists, were delighted that the Capuchin could be trained to do all these things. But in order to do so, they had to remove the monkey's teeth to stop it biting the man, and then tie an electric shock pack to its body so that further aggression towards him could be arrested whenever it was exhibited. Not a very successful experiment, if you ask me!

Any veterinarian will tell you that year by year the number of mice, rats, gerbils, hamsters and guinea-pigs brought to the clinic is increasing. Why have we taken so long to look upon these creatures as domestic pets? Probably because the electric light is such a relatively new device. Most of these rodents are nocturnal, and it has only been since the general usage of artificial light that we have been able to keep them as pets. Although they admirably fulfil our need for "warm furries", their soiling habits, mean that we must usually keep them, like birds, in closed environments. Because of this there is less physical contact, and certainly no greeting at the door, although they also are less at risk of being scrunched underfoot.

No, dogs and cats have it right. They are neither too small nor too large. Their odours, although sometimes overwhelming are, in good health, not disagreeable, Their specialized eating and toilet habits meet with our needs. They were in the right place at the right time. And the dog, in particular, had such an excitingly great genetic flexibility that we were able to shrink or enlarge it physically to meet our needs and wants without dramatically changing its basic wolf-inherited behaviour. Right now there is nothing else on the market that comes close. The dog and cat are two success stories, and it appears that they will continue as such in the foreseeable future.

CHAPTER TWO

Pets, health and humour

I was in Philadelphia recently, on my own, attending a scientific meeting. The university put me up at the local Holiday Inn, and on the first morning I went to the restaurant for breakfast. Having only arrived the night before from London, I did not feel like having a large breakfast. My waitress arrived and, in the warm way of American waitresses, welcomed me and asked me if I was ready to order. I reciprocated her warmth and asked for half a melon and a cup of coffee. "That's no breakfast, honey!" she told me, loud enough for all nearby tables to hear. "Look at you. You're too thin, honey. You need something good for you. Let me get you some eggs and bacon and hashbrowns." And she was off! Was this new Holiday Inn policy, to be implemented from Duluth to Dubai? Did one of the executives of the hotel own a poultry farm? Were the waitresses on a profit sharing plan? No. None of that. This sweet, black, middle-aged Philadelphian simply couldn't help it. She needed to nurture. And I, sitting alone, probably looking a little ill at ease, gave her a suitable subject. If I were a Golden Retriever and she were a pet owner her response might well have been the same. We all need to nurture, and at some times in our lives, we need to do a lot of nurturing.

The human has a varied repertoire of needs and behaviours which we share with most other mammals. Hunger, sex, aggression, territoriality, dominance and exploration are common needs, but social animals, like the human or the canine or the feline, have one more piece of behaviour crucial to their success, and that is called attachment.

Attachment is normal evolutionary behaviour. It has evolved to protect us from the cold, from hunger and from predators. Attachment is the evolutionary behaviour of the young. The complementary behaviour of the parent is care-giving or nurturing. That is what I was getting from my waitress in Philadelphia, and that is what I see my clients giving to my patients. Nurturing or care-giving is the basis for the relationship between people and pets today, but first let me describe a little more about the theory of attachment behaviour.

Attachment begins with touch, the frequent touch between the baby and the mother. Once the infant can focus its eyes, eye contact is made and the baby will mimic its mother's facial movements. But touch is still the most important. We all know that crying, for example, stops when physical contact is given. Attachment between infant and mother will soon generalize to father and to siblings. Eventually, attachment behaviour will extend to the extended family, to peer groups (whether they realize it or not, all vets are attached to each other), and to male/female relationships.

Put simply, in infancy the baby is an object of care. Attachment is synonymous with nurture. In adulthood there is a role reversal. The adult manifests his or her need for attachment by being a source for nurture. I like feeding my dog. I like brushing her. I feel satisfied by caring for her.

Attachment is not without risks, however. Making attachments involves loving. Breaking attachments produces grief. Attachments put at risk, for example, through the hospitalization of a seriously ill pet, can produce anxiety, sorrow or anger. Fear of the loss of attachment, fear of separation, can result in compulsive care-giving or a clinging, over-dependent relationship. I will explain some of the problems inherent in attachment in chapters 5 and 6, but first let us look at what some psychiatrists say about attachment between people and pets.

Alasdair MacDonald, a psychiatrist in Somerset, has written "Pets are less threatening and more controllable than human attachment figures. At the same time, the combined qualities of warmth, touch, non-threatening movement and sound produce a simple analogue of human attachment behaviour."

Dr E. K. Rynearson, a psychiatrist in the western United States, has said "The exchange of acceptance and affection between us and pets is less complicated than human exchange of similar need and satisfaction." Freud called this relationship "affection without ambivalence". Kenneth Keddie in Scotland has written that "animals bolster the pet owner's morale and remind him that he is, in fact, a special and unique individual", while Dr A. Siegal in the eastern United States has written "The animal does not judge but offers a feeling of intense loyalty; it does not expose its master to the ugly strain of constant criticism. It provides its owner with a chance to feel important."

Non-threatening . . . controllable . . . warm . . . less complicated . . . morale boosting . . . intensely loyal . . . it sounds as though pets are a panacea for all the ills of mankind. They are not. Far from it. But there must be something unique in the relationship between people and pets, something not found in the relationship between people and people, to explain these things.

James Thurber said that he always thought that a dog lover was a dog in love with another dog. He's right, of course. I see a lot of them. They prance into the clinic as if on roller skates, self-confident and defiant. "I'm the local stud", they seem to be saying, "and don't you forget it." But there is obviously more to it than that. Let us look at the relationship between people and pets and see if it can explain the close, loving attachment that some people have with their animals.

Constance Perin is a cultural anthropologist who lives in New England and who has articulated, perhaps better than anyone else, a plausible explanation of the symbolic role pets play in our lives. Starting with attachment theory, Perin has written how the life-long "puppy" in dogs – the licking, the nuzzling, the pleasurable sounds, the tail and body wagging, the submissive gestures – are all releasers for our inherent nurturing behaviour. These things bring out the parent in us. At the same time, as she points out, it is widely accepted that dogs can serve as transitional objects providing warmth and security in the same sense that teddy bears and security blankets do. But this then creates a dilemma, for a transitional object symbolically, and Perin is only speaking symbolically, represents mother. In other words, the animal stimulates an ambivalent response. It stimulates the "mother" in us while at the same time acting as a transitional object. We mother them and they mother us.

The bond between mother and infant is unique in one's lifetime. It is a time of unquestioning devotion, an absence of judging, total trust, unspoken understanding and unbounded love. It has been described as a time when mother and infant are merged. But "merger with mother" must end. Mothers instinctively know this. Cats lose interest in their kittens as they mature, but they do so at a time co-ordinated with the kittens' ability to find food on their own.

We do the same. Growing up means breaking bonds. It begins with moving away and exploring, then returning. My youngest daughter, Tamara, at six, goes off and explores, but when uncertain does what all six-year-olds do. She cuts off the circulation in my leg by clinging.

The intimacy of infancy is a time of perfection. But development brings with it separation and independence. The idyllic state between the infant and mother can never be repeated in any other bond with a human being. The trust, the adoration, the "superabundant love" as Perin calls it, is a once-in-a-lifetime experience. But it is an experience that we subconsciously remember and symbolically the dog can be a vehicle for that memory. "Speechless . . ., yet communicating perfectly, the mute and ever-attentive dog portrays our own memory of that once in a lifetime bond."

If that is the case, then it explains something that has troubled me since I started practice. Occasionally, someone will tell me, usually self-consciously, almost always apologetically, "I love my dog more than my children." Now, I have a dog and I have three children. I love my dog very much. She, in fact, could be said to be directly responsible for the children, for it was through her that I met my wife. But if it ever came to a choice between her and the children it's no contest. The children are my children. They are my genes and I will protect them. The dog is a gorgeous, gentle thing, but she is a dog. Yet people really mean it when they tell me they love their dogs more than their children. They tell me with intent and with seriousness. And they are otherwise sensible sound people. Perin's explanation of the dual role that pets play, that of something to care for yet something that offers comfort and security, gives me at least a theoretically plausible explanation for the statement. Some people

"I love my dog more than my children"

find it difficult to exist without the presence of super-abundant love as there was in infancy, even if it is a facsimile. The pet dog's unmitigated response and affection perhaps fill a void that no human attachment could fill.

Constance Perin speaks from the anthropologists' view, and rightly sees the dog in western society as a cultural phenomenon. After all, dog is still eaten in many parts of Asia. The bond we have developed with them, in Europe and the Americas, is cultural not biological, but is there such a thing as a biological bond?

Several years ago, in the cardiac intensive care unit of a Maryland hospital, an intriguing scientific observation was made by sheer fluke. A psychiatrist was standing at the nurse's station where such vital signs as electrocardiograph pattern are monitored, when he noticed that, in sequence around the ward and for very short lengths of time, each patient's heart rhythm temporarily improved. By back-tracking he discovered that this coincided with the duty nurse checking each patient's pulse. (Why their pulses were being checked when they were already attached to every tube and electrode known to science, I really don't know.)

This was a fascinating observation. The mere touch of a nurse's hand on the patient's wrist was sufficient to have a beneficial physiological effect. It was a fact with extremely important implications, not the least important being the question of whether the very set-up of an intensive care unit was deleterious to the patient's health. But let's look at this only from the point of pet ownership.

It has been known for some time that stroking a pet dog reduces that dog's blood pressure, although there are still those who would criticize this statement. Medical tradition has always dictated that, if the body's activity is to be studied, the subjects should be isolated from unwanted effects of their environments. Freud used hypnosis; Pavlov put his animal subjects in boxes. That scientific tradition is still with us today but, in the history of pet research, it had a particularly perverse consequence. James Lynch and Aaron Katcher, two psychiatrists at the University of Pennsylvania, wanted to study the effect of stroking and petting on a dog's blood pressure. When asked to comment on the experiment design, their graduate students asked, "But what about the differences in the ways people stroke dogs?" Their solution? The students suggested putting the dog in an enclosed empty room and then, with a long pole attached to various gizmos, reaching in and stroking the dog with uniform pressure and movement. This, they said, would eliminate the variables that would occur if different people stroked the dog. It would also, of course, eliminate the very interaction that they wished to study.

The fact was, however, statistically established. Stroking a dog reduced its blood pressure. Now Lynch and Katcher wanted to turn the tables. They wanted to see if there were any changes to the "stroker".

This is easier said than done. Katcher and Lynch wanted to monitor resting blood pressure levels in pet owners, and then observe any changes that might occur when the owners greeted their animals and petted them.

For all of his fascinating research, Aaron Katcher suffers from one major deficit. He does not own a pet, and because he does not own a pet, he did not know what any pet owner knows; that the experiment was doomed to failure. We don't just sit there when we greet our own pets. We rub them. We talk to them. We tickle them. We ask them how they are. We are too active with them for Katcher's experiment to be used. Katcher and his graduate students discovered the problem inherent in their experiment design very quickly, and modified it to include both talking and touching.

James Lynch had previously studied the effect of talking on blood pressure because he wanted to understand more about the stresses of talking – after all, one of the frequent complaints within marriages is a lack of ability to talk about things. As a result, he knew that when his subjects read aloud or spoke their blood pressure rose, and that when they rested or were spoken to their blood pressure fell. He also knew that the higher the subjects' resting blood pressure was, the greater the rise would be when that person spoke. What was actually said in the conversation did not affect the changes.

They now repeated this experiment, but this time had the talker greet and touch his or her own dog. When these pet animals were both greeted and petted, the owner's blood pressure actually dropped below the resting level. This not only meant that greeting and stroking a pet was less stressful than talking to another human, it meant that greeting and talking to pets was physiologically good for you, especially if you suffered from high blood pressure to begin with.

Lynch and Katcher, however, could not determine from the experiment whether it was the talking or the touching, or the seeing for that matter, which was beneficial, so they set up several more experiments.

Being logical people, they, and a colleague, Alan Beck, decided that of the various common pets, the ones least likely to be stroked and petted were fish. They also thought that it was unlikely that tropical fish were spoken to with any great frequency. I am occasionally brought a sick goldfish or black molly (in fact, one of my most satisfying cases involved curing a hybrid goldfish with ulcers on both eyes by changing its bowl from circular to rectangular, thus saving its eyes from rubbing against the glass as it swam round and round); but I would agree that fish owners really don't talk to and touch their fish as much as other pet owners; that, of course, is a presumption on my part as well.

Individuals in this study were asked to read aloud, and then relax for ten minutes by looking at a bare wall. At the end of that time, they were to look at a tropical fish tank. What was observed was that, when they looked at the tropical fish swimming in the tank, their blood pressure dropped. When they were asked to read aloud afterwards, their blood

pressure did not go as high as it went when they read aloud before the experiment. This finding was consistent with two other facts. It was known that a child performing tests in an experimenter's living room had a lower blood pressure when a dog was present than when a dog was not present. And it was also known that a child's blood pressure, which would usually go up when reading aloud, would actually go down when reading aloud in the presence of a dog. This meant that, aside from talk and touch, seeing a pet and being in its presence had beneficial effects on heart function.

For some reason, communication in the presence of an animal was less stressful even when there was no talking or touching of the animal. My clients are always touching their pets and talking to them, and I have noticed that if I have to give difficult news or advice to an owner, I touch my dog, an old lady who has taken to living beside my desk in her later years, while I speak.

Katcher then set up an experiment based on observation. Using a graduate student trained in the study of behaviour, and a stooge dog, a Golden Retriever named Emily, he arranged that this couple sit in the reception room at the University of Pennsylvania's Animal Hospital waiting room. There the observer sat and observed. She watched people finger their pets, stroke them, fondle them, pet them, kiss them, cuddle them, massage them, tickle them, pat them, scratch them, groom them and do everything else that we do with them. But she observed scientifically.

Her first observation was that men stroke, fondle, scratch, tickle and cuddle their pets as much as women. There was no difference in either the manner or the frequency. Now, it has been suggested that men in Western society have less need for affection, and certainly in public we kiss and cuddle less than women do. Could it be that pets are for us a culturally acceptable medium for the physical contact we instinctively or physiologically need or want, and that pets are a means through which we can show and give affection in public situations?

The species of pet is also concerned in this question, because there seems to be a cultural bias in Britain and North America against men owning cats. This may change in the future as the cat continues its increase in popularity, but at present the majority of the cats I see that are owned by people living alone are owned by women. In a survey in Toronto, over 90% of cats in apartments were owned by women. It may be that a woman's need to nurture blossoms earlier in life, and that men simply don't want to be encumbered with the responsibility of caring for a cat. But I see a reverse within the homosexual pet-owning population. In that group, in London, the cat appears to be the favoured species of pet amongst male homosexuals. I don't know why this is.

The second observation was that the size of dog did not matter. People fiddled with their Dandy Dinmonts as much as with their Rotweilers! The researcher's third observation was the most important. She observed what Katcher called "idle play". Idle play occurs when the owner and the pet are in contact with each other but do not have each other's attention. The owner is not looking at the dog. The dog is not soliciting attention. The owner may, in fact, be doing something else, as I am doing when I talk to someone and stroke my Golden Retriever at the same time. Idle play can take any form. It can involve stroking, patting, scratching, ruffling or smoothing the fur, or grooming. One lady I know always squeezes her dog's sebaceous cysts while she is talking to me.

We create a kind of intimacy when we do these things which is enormously comforting. We are reducing our state of arousal. We are reducing our blood pressure. We are fulfilling our most primitive and basic need, the need to touch. Men in the Middle East do the same with their worry beads. People in California and New York may do it through group contact therapy. The very word that we use in English to describe the companion animal, "pet", probably tells as much about the central role that dogs and cats play as anything else.

My nurses and I started to pay more attention to what our clients did with our patients, either in the reception room or in the consulting/examining room.

A visit to the veterinarian is a stress-inducing exercise. Even if the visit is only for a preventive vaccination, the owner will worry that the injection will hurt. It claws are to be cut, there is the worry that the animal may not behave. If the animal is brought in because it is not well, then of course there is the worry that it is terribly unwell. Unfortunately, there is one more worry; a hangover from the past in veterinary medicine. That is the worry that if the pet is terribly unwell, the veterinarian will kill it because "nothing can be done". It's a big worry. Almost every day someone will bring in his or her pet, an animal suffering from itchy skin, diarrhoea, a lump in the skin, and will ask "Will he have to be put down?" Veterinary medicine still has that cachet, and if that doesn't induce stress in owners, then they are made of stone. It certainly stresses the veterinarian.

The owner copes by doing a number of things. The smoker smokes, although my request not to smoke in my office stifles that outlet. Usually more than one person accompanies the owner; 1·6 people, according to an American survey. They bring tidbits to give their pets. But most important, they touch their pets. If the dog is small enough, it will be on a lap. The owner might be talking to the nurse or someone else. She might be looking out of the window to check on the traffic warden situation, but she will, almost absently, be petting the dog. Naturally, she is doing it for the dog, but she is doing it for herself as well. This is Katcher's "idle play".

In the examining room a history is taken, usually with the owner sitting down, and "idle play" continues. The animal is put on the examining table, but here an interesting thing happens. Over 80% of the time the owner picks up the dog with the dog's head to the owner's left. If the dog is facing the other way, owners will move themselves around so that they still pick their dogs up this way. I thought that the position of the examining table might have led to this, so I moved it and reversed the situation. Yet owners still picked their dogs up with the head to the left. My only explanation for this is that it is another manifestation of the owner's instinctive nurturing of the pet. Mothers will usually cradle infants with the infant's head on the left, near the heart. It seems that pet owners do the same.

Once the animal has been examined, there may be a need to discuss the situation. Once more, the owner will absently

groom, stroke and massage the pet while I explain. This is
the situation in which I find that, if I have to explain a
condition where the prognosis is grave or hopeless, I reach
down and stroke my Golden Retriever. I do it in these
circumstances more than the owners. I'm doing it for me,
not for my dog.

All of this is in a clinical situation, but stroking a pet,
talking to it and looking at it, probably have a stress relieving
effect in the home as well. If so, this would explain an
intriguing fact that emerged from a study of survivability one
year after a major heart attack in patients who were treated in
a cardiac intensive care unit.

The research was initiated because, in previous work,
James Lynch and others before him had observed that the
married lived longer than the single, widowed or divorced.
The researcher, Erica Friedmann, wanted to investigate the
effect of social isolation on death rates in people who had
been hospitalized for severe heart disease. Friedmann designed a project that looked primarily at the impact of human
relationships, but amongst her fifty or so items relating to
social support and isolation, she included a question on pet
ownership. Her results showed that, out of all the items in
the questionnaire, it was pet ownership which proved the
strongest social predictor of survival for one year after
hospital treatment. Her statistics are interesting, and are as
follows:

PATIENTS	PET	NO PET	TOTAL
Alive	50	28	78
Not alive	3	11	14
Total	53	39	92

Well, this is pretty strange stuff. Own a pet and live longer?
It sounds like a put-on.

The researchers started looking at all the variables involved, or rather the computer did. They saw that this
greater survivability of pet owners was not related to the
patient's better health at the start of the study. It was not due

to better social status. It was not even due to the exercise that dog owners get through exercising their dogs. Cat owners had as great a chance of being alive one year after their heart attacks as did dog owners. Most important, this greater chance of survival was not only present amongst the socially isolated; those who were to be studied in the first place. It was there in married people and in others who had good social support. It meant that there are possible benefits from association with pets which are independent of, and perhaps supplementary to, the benefits of human contact. These could be the talking to, the touching and the looking at animals that I previously described. We know that these things have a physiological effect on the body. They reduce blood pressure, especially in those suffering from high blood pressure. They reduce the state of arousal. But there is another fact that this research failed to look at, and which I think is vital to an understanding of why we keep pets. They make us laugh.

Samuel Butler said, "The great pleasure of a dog is that you may make a fool of yourself with him, and not only will he not scold you, but he will make a fool of himself too." I think that this is central to the enjoyment of keeping pets. The more I see them, treat them and hear their owners talk about them, the more I am convinced that their main role is to provide play and enjoyment, which also means amusement and laughter.

Leo Bustad, the Dean of Washington State University, says his dog's name is "Dingbat". When I asked why (dingbat means crazy), he said, "I call 'em the way I see 'em". Names carry all kinds of associations with them. The name that an owner gives a pet can indicate the direction that that animal's life will take. The name can say something about the owner's ambitions for the pet. It almost always indicates what role the pet is expected to fulfil.

Many years ago, a retired British diplomat brought his two Pug dogs, Emma and Cabot, to the surgery where I was working at the time. After a few visits, I asked him one day why he picked those names. Pugs, in my experience, are usually called Doncaster or Thrumpington. Emma and

Emma and Cabot

Cabot didn't sound right. He told me that when he was on diplomatic posting to the United States he and his wife became close friends with the American diplomat, Henry Cabot Lodge, and his wife, Emma. He said that the Cabot Lodge's were delightful; as warm and as generous a couple as he would ever know. They were, however, "very American. Once they started talking there was no possibility of stopping them." When he returned to Britain, he named his newly-acquired pets Cabot and Emma. He did so out of affection for his friends. He also did so because, whenever the dogs barked, he got a vicarious thrill out of shouting, "Shut up, Cabot! Shut up, Emma!"

In 1942, a researcher named Nathan Shoenfeld examined reactions to peoples names. He observed that Mary was thought to be quiet, Edward was friendly, Richard was good looking, Barbara was charming and Adrian was artistic. These were subjective reactions to names. We all react to names. We make immediate initial judgements.

The usage of names is constantly changing. Today, a "Y" ending to a name is strongly associated with girls' names. Ten years ago, some research showed that people thought that Dave was strong and active, but that Davey was weak and passive. This type of sexism occurs in pets' names as well. Fancy spellings are almost invariably given to female names (females are frivolous). Male animals' names are always spelt in a straight-forward manner (males are straight and to the point). Both of these facts show clearly in the names given to pets. Consider the following names:

Mutley	Chewy	Toby	Billy
Noddy	Conky	Snoopy	Ricky
Dandy	Charlie	Sandy	Sammy

All of these are male dogs. Mutley is a West Highland
Terrier, Sandy is a Labrador, Dandy is a Lhasa Apso, Toby is
an Old English Sheepdog, Ricky is a Yorkshire Terrier,
Charlie is an Alsatian. They are all different breeds and sizes,
but their names give a clue to one common denominator.
Regardless of breed, they have been "feminized". They have
been "feminized" to the sex stereotype of being passive and
friendly. When I am told that the next patient is an Alsatian
named Charlie my reaction is different to what it would be if
he were named Bruiser. Now look at the following names:

Tryna
Mitzy ("make sure you spell it with a 'y'")
Bar-Bee
Saydie
Hunney
Suzann

All of these names belong to females. Tryna is a Pekingese,
Mitzy is a Poodle, Bar-Bee is a Chihuahua, Saydie is a Shih
Tzu. They are all small breeds. The deliberate exoticism of
their names says something about the owners. The names
indicate the importance of the pet to the owner. The names
show that deliberation has been involved. They give a
suggestion that these dogs will be pampered. The veterinarian understands what type of person owns the dog, and
what his or her needs are, simply by seeing that a name is
spelled in an unusual manner.

Pets are frequently given descriptive names. Trouble is a
Dachshund, Flash a Dalmatian, Dizzie an Irish Setter and
Treacle a Poodle. The names may be descriptive of the
physical attributes of the pet. One of my favourite patients
was Grot, a Yorkshire Terrier. Another was Scruffy; the
same breed. Frizzy is a Fox Terrier, Jet a black Labrador,
Cadbury a brown Poodle and Rags is an Australian Terrier.
Itch is a gerbil. Owners frequently choose names that denote
the origin of the breed, or at least what they believe the origin
to be. Poodles frequently get French names, although the
breed, in fact, originated in Germany. Lhasa Apsos are called
Sherpa. West Highland Terriers are called Angus, Scottish
Terriers are called Heather or MacDuff. Dachshunds are
named Heinz and Sigmund.

Pets' names can sometimes give a clue to the owner's occupation. Ben and Truman are two pub cats. Vodka is a pub Alsatian. Gielgud is a Dalmatian owned by an actor. Sir John himself has a Shi Tzu named Chester, which he acquired when he was playing at Chichester, and a Pekingese named Caesar, given to him when he starred in the film of that play.

Inversion of names is common, perhaps more so with small pets. Hercules is a Yorkshire Terrier, Spartacus is a gerbil, Hannibal is a hamster.

Pets are, of course, given names for a variety of reasons, and in fact the owner has more freedom to express him or herself in naming a pet than in naming a child. Pets are named after heroes: Elvis, Dylan, Streisand, Frodo. They can suffer the "Walt Disney" effect: Bambi, Heidi, Dopy, Grumpy. They can become cartoon characters. I see many black and white cats named Sylvester, and Snoopy is the most common name of all for dogs of all sizes and descriptions.

The pet's name can suggest the political or philosophical leanings of the owners: Mao, Che, Plato, Thatcher. (Actually, Thatcher is a cat who is booted out of the house each time the economic news worsens.) Pets are named after incidents. Wednesday is a Yorkshire Terrier purchased you know when. Toosoon, a Poodle, was bought too soon after the death of the previous pet. George, a female cat, is named after George a male rabbit that the owner had when he was a child.

Historically in Britain, the upper classes used surnames for all but intimate and personal conversation. Use of first names was restricted to the lower classes. Similarly, the terms Mr and Mrs were used by polite society. It was formal and proper to do so. These facts have their manifestation today in pets' names. The role that a family wants Perkins to play is different from that expected of Dave. Mr Pim will probably be given more independence than Cuddles. Rank is frequently given with names, and with it, authority. Duke and King are undoubtedly dogs to respect.

In looking through the names of pets I have seen, one fact emerges. Fashionable names for people are not fashionable for pets. In 1978, in the UK, the most common names for male babies were Stephen, Mark, Paul and Andrew. I don't think I've ever met a pet with any of those names. My patients are called Rupert, Horatio, Hubert, Bertha, Emma, Nellie. They are given dated names. Is it nostalgia? I think so. They speak for a lost heritage. They are given old-fashioned flower names, like Petunia, and jewel names like Ruby; names that our grandparents and great-grandparents might have had. And in that way, the names of pets indicate the role that they are coming to play. We yearn for the "order" of the past, where virtue was admired, beauty was respected and our position in the order of things was known. We give our pets names that remind us of an age when such things were so.

Pets' names fulfil perhaps their most important role in permitting their owners to use either nicknames or lovenames publicly. Read the names in *The Times*' Valentine's Day classified ads. It seems that half the ads are placed by dogs. Fuzzypeg, BooBabe, Snuffit, Daffodil, Tweetiepie, Pussywillow, Twinkletoes, Bugga-Poo, Sunshine, Angel, Treasure, Cupid. Pets' names are frequently "release" names. They are frequently diminutives. They are often based on baby language and carry the suggestion of parenthood and of intimacy. They are names of affection or love which we would be embarrassed to use in public with our close friends, but which society finds acceptable to use publicly for pets.

In a similar fashion, dogs and cats are commonly given role names. Dogs are given names for roles the owners wish them to fulfil. Cats, because they are cats, are given names which often describe their character.

Consider the following:

Vicious	Strangeways
Fang	Slasher
Dumbo	Scatty
Bananas	Kissin
Bandit	Spunky
Spike	Sunshine
The Fonz	Squeak
Bugs	Grumpy
Dread	Mischief

Dread   Grumpy

These are all cats; those on the left are male and on the right female.

The following are dogs' names, again with males on the left and females on the right:

Sweetie	Blossom
Blitz	Princess
Sunshine	Beauty
Flash	Baby
Victor	Precious
Napoleon	Serene
Genghis	Treasure
Rebel	Angel

The names indicate the roles these animals are expected to play. My favourite is a black cat belonging to a young man who had just left home and was living on his own for the first time. He calls his cat Mom.

Names of certain pets remain with me because they are either so aptly descriptive of the animal, or because of their wit. As with most pets' names, they show an element of fun. I have made a list of some of them:

Capone – *a delinquent Dobermann*

Spike – *a hedgehog*

Crazy Joe – *a terrapin*

Ruff and Tumble – *two Dachshunds*

Kinky – *a male Poodle with an obsession with cushions*

Burp – *an embarrassing Weimaraner*

Enoch – *a Dandy Dinmont who didn't feel comfortable with blacks*

Yoyo – *a nutty Shi Tzu*

Splodge – *a laid-back Golden Retriever*

Pussywillow – *a serene grey cat*

Flaky – *a cat that hallucinates (so it seems)*

Calpurnia – *a Persian cat with the loudest purr in London*

Oedipus, a kitten who wouldn't leave his mother

I know of one Labrador pup that recently carried a waterhose from the back garden into its home while the owners were absent. It caused thousands of pounds worth of damage, but when the owners told me about it, they only laughed. "At least its done one thing", they said. "We were having trouble picking a name for her, but she's done that herself. We're going to call her Flood."

It is not only the names that owners choose for their pets that have humorous connotations. Owners can see humour in almost any pet activity. Admittedly, sex in any species of animal, including us, is funny when you consider the physical requirements and dexterity necessary, but it is one area of unbridled amusement for many owners, probably because of the serious intent on the part of the pet in the incongruous situation in which it usually takes place. It reminds me of the cartoon of a male dog, latched on to the leg of a guest as the visitor has walked through the front door of a house, which is captioned, "He's really taken to you, hasn't he?"

The amusement that pets provide is not restricted to intermittent activity. It is there in their day-to-day behaviour. I have, in my desk, a series of photos which were given to me late last year. A very proper, middle-aged lady, a client of mine for some years, dropped them in. "I've got something to show you that only you will understand," I remember her telling me. The brightness of her eyes lit up the room as she handed me the photos. When I looked at them I saw nothing but a brown blur on a beige background. "It's the wall of death," she said.

"What?"

"The wall of death. He's doing the wall of death. He does it for me every night, and last week I took these pictures."

I looked again, concentrating, and this time fantasized that the brown blur was her cat Jaws.

"But what is he on?" I asked. I could not discern what he was walking on.

"Why, it's hessian," she replied, assuming that I knew the cat was on the wall and only wanted to know the quality of the wallpaper. "He only does the wall of death on hessian. Isn't he funny? And he's so serious when he does it."

It was only then obvious that she was showing me photographs of her cat running around the room . . . on the walls. The hessian wallpaper was in tatters, but never mind. The cat was amusing her. It was making her feel good. The very fact that the cat was not actually doing it to amuse her, but was doing it "seriously" made it even more amusing. It took me back to university where as a student I had a cat which did what I guess I should now call "the corridor of death". My two room-mates and I would settle down after dinner to watch our grey tabby cat purposefully walk to the front door, sit down, look back through the living room down the straight corridor to the bathroom at the end and then, as if shot from a cannon, fly like a missile down the corridor, putting the brakes on only as it hit the bath mat, hitting the bathtub with a force that one thought would fracture the porcelain. And we would roll on the floor with laughter. The tabby would reverse the procedure, this time sliding on the front door mat into the door itself, causing a hollow thud that could be heard in all the other flats on our floor. This was our evening ritual. We waited for the cat to amuse us before we started our evening's bookwork. It was as if this amusement revitalized us for the work ahead.

Norman Cousins, the former Editor of the American magazine *Saturday Review*, wrote a perceptive little book a few years ago, which he called *Anatomy of an Illness as Perceived by the Patient*. He described the role of laughter in helping him to reduce the amount of pain that he was experiencing because of a crippling disease. Cousins felt that everything about his condition and treatment was depressing and that if he were depressed, he knew his chances of recovery were diminished. As editor of the *Saturday Review*, and with a special interest in medicine, he was aware of the statistics and reports that showed that people suffering from depression had a greater incidence of all diseases, including cancer and heart disease. He decided to rectify the situation as best he could. First he hired a nurse to tell him jokes. The only drawback to this, he reported, was that his laughter programme was disturbing the other patients in the hospital. Next, he booked himself out of the hospital and into a hotel. He says this made him feel great because he was saving so much money. In the hotel, Cousins continued his regimen of watching old Marx Brothers' films and having jokes told to him. He went on to say that his blood sedimentation rate, a measure of the inflammatory process that affected him, gradually diminished as a consequence of his systematic programme of introducing laughter into his therapy.

The theoretical basis for Cousins' beliefs is quite simple. It has been known for years that the state of depression is related to chemical changes in the brain. These chemicals are beginning to be understood, which is why, in the last decade, such chemicals as "anti-depressants" have been available for the treatment of depression. If there are chemicals known to cause depression, and depression is related to a greater incidence and severity of disease, can it not logically be argued that the state of happiness and laughter is also a chemical state and that these chemical changes in the body are good for you?

Nothing of importance in evolution develops without a reason. Laughter and a sense of humour are evolutionary developments in all groups of humans. They are there for a purpose, and the core of our genetic purpose is to perpetuate our genes. In other words, laughter and humour are there to help us survive. Almost without doubt, the chemical basis for these feelings will be discovered in the next decade. In the meantime, the feeling of amusement and humour that many pets give to their owners probably has a sound physiological benefit. Watch Fido tear a slipper apart and live longer?

CHAPTER THREE

The emotional bond

Sarah Miles, the excellent British actress, returned to Britain two years ago to work here professionally for the first time in years. Naturally, she was interviewed on the Michael Parkinson Show. Those who saw the programme might remember that she appeared with her dog, and that the dog got quite a bit of attention from her. In fact, her sequence on the programme could be used as an educational film in explaining the bond between people and their pets. It certainly exemplified the emotional security that a pet provides. In fact, let's compare Michael Parkinson with Miss Miles's Skye Terrier. Miss Miles spoke to both of them on the programme.

The Skye Terrier is "pre-verbal". It is like an infant in that sense, and because it is "preverbal" there is, of course, no chance of a verbal misunderstanding between them. Notwithstanding the jokes, Michael Parkinson is verbal and it must certainly be the guest's constant dread on programmes such as this that they put what they want to say incorrectly or are misunderstood.

Miss Miles touched her dog frequently during the interview. We all have a craving for closeness and we know the physiological benefits we get from stroking a pet. Pets are symbolically imbued with a warm, trusting, and unconditional caring that satisfies our need for closeness. Michael Parkinson may well fill that requirement for many of his viewers, but unfortunately our culture does not permit Miss Miles to stroke him on nationwide television.

During her interview, Miss Miles looked directly at her

dog. Sometimes people will hold their dog's head steady so that there is direct eye to eye contact. You can do it because there is no threat involved. Try doing it with another human, however. A wealth of emotions come into play. We avert our eyes eventually. It is easier to gaze into your Terrier's eyes than into Michael Parkinson's eyes.

Miss Miles carried her pet. The dog was subordinate and controllable. But the programme she was on was Mr Parkinson's and by definition he must be the opposite.

Many people look on their pets as confidants

Miss Miles's pet was, as most owners feel, non-threatening and a source of unconditional love. Mr Parkinson may well be both, but not in his position as interviewer.

Many people look on their pet dogs and cats as confidants. The fact that Sarah Miles brought the dog on to the programme implies that it must be a "friend". Although the objective of such programmes is that the guests confide in the interviewer, Michael Parkinson is still, regardless of the sympathy he might show, performing an inquisition. He is drawing information out of his guests.

All of this can be grouped under one fact. Sarah Miles had her pet dog on the programme for emotional security. There is nothing wrong with this. It is, in fact, one of the major reasons we keep pets. For many reasons, pets can sometimes

provide easier emotional security than can people. Miss Miles
has certainly had far more than her fair share of personal
problems in her life, and it could well be that she has
developed an apprehension, or even a distrust at present, of
human attachments. If that were the case, her normal need
for attachment could be displaced to her pet. After all, the
Skye Terrier is receptive to it and, most important, unconditional. It makes for a happy, alive and reciprocal
relationship.

The emotional security that a pet can provide is not
restricted to the needs of expatriate British actresses returning
home. It can exist in many societies and cultures. The
Athabaskan Hare Indians in the Canadian North West
Territories are a case in point.

Anthropologists who have observed the Colville Lake
tribe have described them as an emotionally repressed,
restrained and contained people, except in one respect. In
their relationship with young children and young pups they
are none of these. Pups are spoiled, indulged, played with,
given choice food, sheltered and rarely punished or scolded.
They are an emotional outlet and objects of pride. They are
cuddled and fondled. Shows of affection with them are
permissible, but only until they mature and become working
animals, at which time affection virtually ceases. But because
there are always pups and children in the community, the
people have an acceptable outlet for natural emotions which
are culturally repressed. Further north in Canada, the dog
sled has been replaced by the snowmobile as the normal
method of winter transportation for the Eskimo. But visit
any Eskimo settlement and you will see that most homes still
keep dogs, often twelve or fourteen. When asked why, the
owners will reply, "We have always kept dogs. It is our way
of life."

An intriguing aspect of the emotional security that pets
provide is what one might call "safety by association". It is
socially permissible to talk to a person with a dog; certainly
more so than talking to a complete stranger. (I am, by the
way, saying this within an urban context. In the country,
certainly in North America, the proscriptions against talking
to strangers are not as great.)

This cultural observation was made by Peter Messent, an animal behaviourist. My veterinary practice is very near Hyde Park in London, and it is in Hyde Park and adjacent Kensington Gardens that many of my clients walk their pets. With their prior approval, Messent followed individual clients from my clinic door, along the street, through the pedestrian underpass and into and around a predetermined circuit within Hyde Park. He furtively followed them, clipboard in hand, fifty yards behind, nipping from tree to tree and noting the reactions of all the people who passed within five feet of the walker. He had each person walk the route alone and then again with his or her dog. Messent observed whether passers-by looked at the dog, looked at the owner, slowed and turned, stopped, talked to the dog, talked to the owner or touched the dog. He kept track of sex (or apparent sex) and the approximate age of the contacts and non-contacts.

His results were not surprising. People walking dogs had more social contacts than the same people walking the same route but not accompanied by dogs. Moreover, when walking dogs, the walk lasted longer.

Passers-by . . .
slowed, turned
stopped

Messent repeated the experiment on a larger scale, but this time taping his observations on a tape recorder. On seven out of ten walks with a dog at least one spoken interaction took place. The average number of spoken interactions per walk was three. Conversations were longer if the other person had a dog as well. People appeared more friendly in the park than on the streets leading to the park.

In other words, people with dogs seem to be more approachable than people without dogs, especially in doggy areas like parks. This is similar to our relationship with children. One may speak to a child in a park without the explicit permission of the child's guardian. And once the child or dog is approached and spoken to, the ice is broken and it is easier, and also now "permissible", to talk to the parent or owner. It is also interesting to note that touching the dog is permissible. Messent observed that 15% of the dogs he watched were touched by strangers. The same is true with babies. Politicians are always kissing babies, but rarely their mothers. Obviously dogs (and probably other animals as well) make people safe to talk to, and it is the image of the dog, or our perception of it, which makes its owner safer, more benign, more approachable and less dangerous. The dog's veterinarian is frequently imbued with this overflow and that is why so many people see their veterinarians as understanding, warm and benign and good confidants.

In every survey that has been taken, the most frequent reason owners give for keeping pets is the companionship they provide. Companionship in this context is almost impossible to define, so let me give you an example.

Let's assume that for centuries your family has lived in the Perigord region of France and has traditionally hunted truffles with the local black and white pig. It is a tradition of centuries, but your dog asks for consideration. Look at the difference between driving to a *truffière* with a 50 lb dog in the back of your car, and with a 400 lb sow. Which animal walks faster and covers more ground? Which animal has a nose sensitive enough to smell only those truffles ripe for harvesting? Which animal hunts for simple pleasure and which one for pure gluttony? Which animal moans and tail-twitches like

Physical attractiveness has a real effect on our attitudes

a worm and tries its hardest to eat the truffle before you get it, and which is happiest with a pat on the head and a morsel of bread? Which animal gives you a lick of thanks for taking it on such an exciting excursion, and which one snorts in indifference? All of this demonstrates the value of the dog as a companion. It works for apparent fun, it works well, it is satisfied with a little contact comfort and a morsel of food. It does not smell offensively. And it eagerly awaits the next *truffière*.

The dog is more a companion than the pig because it is also more attractive to us, it gives us more praise, and it is more competent at its job.

Physical attractiveness has a real effect on our attitudes. We like people who are physically attractive. Karen Dion, a social psychologist at the University of Toronto, has found this to be true not only in adults but in children at four and five years of age. What is more interesting is that there is evidence that we attribute less blame to the physically attractive, regardless of the facts. I think we do the same with pets.

Dion examined the idea this way. Women were given reports of fairly severe classroom misbehaviour and attached to each report was a photo of the child involved. Some of these photos were of attractive children and some of physically unattractive girls or boys. The women generally placed more blame on the unattractive children. Disruptive behaviour allegedly carried out by the attractive child was usually excused, even when it was exactly the same as the criticized behaviour of the unattractive child.

Our response to dogs and cats is just the same. Simply because they are what they are – furry, large-eyed and visually appealing – we tend to excuse crimes against the household that we would never permit our children to perpetrate. Just yesterday, while giving a final vaccination to a Labrador pup, its owner told me that it had, that morning, eaten a £20 note. "But why didn't you phone me?" I said, "I could have got it back for you simply by giving an injection." "Oh, but he's so beautiful," was the reply, and the pup was given a Mary Quant Deadly Nightshade kiss on his head, a mark of love which he will carry until it rains. I should point out that there is a limit, however, with most owners. Several years ago I was awakened at 2.00 a.m. by an irate and anxious owner who's pup had just eaten a roll of ten £20 notes. "I don't care if you have to slit the bugger from stem to stern," he said, "I just want my bloody money back." Two hundred pounds would have bought a whole litter of pups at that time.

We are attracted to the dog by its physical attractiveness, but also because it gives us praise. Dale Carnegie, in his book *How to Win Friends and Influence People*, said "dole out praise lavishly". This book appears to have been compulsory reading for generations of dogs. People like being liked. But what is more, the greater a person's insecurity and self-doubt, the fonder that person will be of the individual who likes him or her. The dog is constantly doling out its apparent love, and in times of stress for the owner the dog can become even more important. Its unquestioning love, its untainted "praise" for its owner fulfils a normal need.

The dog's and cat's competence at what they do is another reason for our being attracted to them. I remember as a child being absolutely amazed at how my Yorkshire Terrier could drink from a bowl without slurping. I remember trying to mimic her and, having failed, being even more incredulous. The Perigord dog off on the *truffière* is attractive because of its competence at working diligently and efficiently. The guide dog leading a blind person is perhaps the most attractive because of its competence in an emotive situation. I see several guide dogs in practice, and I like them all, but there is one, that I don't see professionally, who is really my favourite.

Four times each day, once in the morning, twice at lunchtime, and again in the late afternoon, a now-ageing Labrador leads its blind owner, at double time, past my house. Over the years it has coped with construction debris, closed footpaths, road works and even bomb damage, and has competently avoided all obstacles to lead its owner safely on his way. And he has done this diligently, professionally, competently and seriously – with a tennis ball in his mouth.

I think he's fantastic. I like him because he is competent. I like him more than the others because he also shows that he is fallible. He is really a dog. Our attitudes towards people are affected in the same way. Elliot Aronson, a social psychologist at the University of Texas showed this to be true

The dog's and cat's competence at what they do is another reason for our being attracted to them

through a simple experiment. Aronson asked subjects to listen to tape recordings of four candidates for an educational quiz. The same actor played all four persons and was –

a) a nearly perfect person,
b) a nearly perfect person who commits a clumsy blunder,
c) a mediocre person, and
d) a mediocre person who commits a clumsy blunder.

The nearly perfect person answers 92% of questions correctly, was an honour student, editor of the yearbook and on the track team. The mediocre person answers 30% of the questions correctly, was an average student, proofread the yearbook and failed to make the track team. The clumsy blunder consisted of sounds of commotion and clatter followed by an anguished voice saying, "Oh my goodness, I've spilled coffee all over my new suit!"

On evaluation, the nearly perfect person who commits a clumsy blunder was found most attractive. He was attractive for spilling his coffee for the same reason that the guide dog is attractive for carrying the tennis ball. Both of these things add an endearing dimension to their characters. We like our perfection tinged with a little human frailty, or in the case of the guide dog, a little canine frailty. It is interesting that in Aronson's study, the least attractive person was the mediocre person who spilled his coffee. This is true of pets as well. The incompetent dog who commits blunders is usually the one who is abandoned or simply allowed to wander. The problem, of course, has its genesis in part in the training it originally got, and is not simply a dog problem but a people problem.

That a large dog provides its owners with a sense of security is not in question. As the incidence of burglary has increased in London, the size of the average dog I see has increased. Both in the UK and in North America in the last decade, the size of the average dog increased. The average dog in California weighed 35% more in 1978 than it did in 1970. Ten years ago I had never seen a Rottweiler. Now I do almost weekly, and I wish I didn't. The present trend both in the United States and in Britain shows that the rapid increase in the ownership of large breeds in the 1970s has reached a plateau.

The owner's attitude towards the protection the dog will give is a web of truth and fantasy, an intrigue of misconceptions, concerning loyalty, and fact, concerning crushing power per square inch of canine jaws.

The truth concerns the large dog's ability to do physical damage. A Rottweiler's jaw can crush an arm. The fantasy concerns the owner's image of the dog, of any family dog, of being loyal unto death. The fantasy image of the dog is of unquestioning love, unchanging, always available, ever loyal. The image is of a loyalty beyond human capacity. We read books and see films devoted to this theme. Almost all of them are fairy tales; make-believe that we want to interpret as true because of the security it gives us.

John Steinbeck is one of the few writers to comment honestly and truthfully. "The human – imperfect and deeply aware of his frailties – is prone to find the virtues he wishes he had in other species – courage in the lion, memory in the elephant, gentleness in the lamb and, oddly enough, both loyalty and honesty in the dog. These are myths which have little basis in fact."

Owners unconsciously intermesh this image of loyalty with protection but they are two totally separate things. I see dogs, and cats for that matter, almost daily who will fight to protect their owners or their owners' homes, but they are not doing it for loyalty. Sex and territory are their imperatives.

Certain breeds, like the Scottish Terrier, are known as "one man dogs", but any dog can develop a possessive attachment to one person. A three-year-old Cavalier King Charles bitch was brought in this week because of increasing protectiveness for its female owner, a protectiveness which has now reached a point where it growls at her husband and children when they come near. I often see dogs that are aggressive with only men, or only women. In fact, sometimes I will see a dog that is down-right too nasty for me to handle other than by brute force, but who will lay his ears back, wag his tail and ask for play from my nurses. Other dogs will be good house dogs. Little or large, they will have a go at strangers' ankles or arms unless they are controlled Their owners appreciate and encourage this, but interpret it wrongly. Although the dog is protecting its territory, the owner sees it as loyalty.

The symbolic role of loyalty that we give dogs must be based on the image we have of them, and that image is based on their behaviour. A dog never grows up. We don't expect it to. We don't expect intellectual development, social conern or moral acuity. It stays the same. It doesn't learn to read or write. It will never know the seven times table. It never learns to tie shoelaces. It never learns to talk or to ride a bicycle. We never allow it to take care of itself. It never learns shame. It is without original sin. It is a constant child, always subordinate to us in a parent-child way. Aaron Katcher describes the dog as a "four-legged Peter Pan, fixed between culture and nature". The child moves from nature to culture, but the dog remains between; neither wolf nor child.

This fixed position, this unchanging role, provides us with a constant factor in our lives. Because the dog does not

Little or large, they will have a go at strangers' ankles

change, we do not have to change in our relation with him. The dog guarantees the continuing presence of the familiar. I am not now the man I was when I married my wife. My wife is not the same person she was then. We are always changing. A good marriage moves with these changes and requires a need to change. My children, of course, change almost monthly.

But our dog, our old Golden Retriever, has remained the same. She is a constant factor, a familiarity, an icon of constancy. And this is what we interpret as loyalty. Her loyalty, which in fables will have her rescuing us from fires and drowning, in truth is simply her constancy. She is an unchanging family member. She might grow old and we might worry about her health, but when she plays she still plays as she did when she was a pup. Her symbolic role of protecting the family is simply a manifestation of her constancy, of her providing us with an unchanging and ever familiar presence.

This familiarity intermingles with another reason we keep pets, and that is the intimacy that they allow us to have with them. Intimacy means many things; closeness, familiarity, warmth. It can be a euphemism for sexual relations, and I do not mean that when I use the term. What I mean is the combination of talking and touching that I have mentioned before. Intimacy involves eye to eye contact, something that may actually be easier to maintain with a dog or cat than with another human. It involves soft touch and quiet talk. It is something that many pet owners feel they have with their pets. It involves sensuality.

Some writers make a silly mistake when they interpret the sensuality in the relationship between people and their pets as sexuality. Iris Nowell, in her book '*The Dog Crisis*' writes, "rubbing the fur of a dog or cat is sexually gratifying to many persons, some of whom reciprocate by masturbating their dogs with about the same nonchalance as picking burrs out of his hair". It is a silly statement because it suggests that stroking or petting an animal, I assume with one's hand, is sexually arousing. If she is talking about stroking or rubbing with the naughty bits, then she has a point, but bestiality, one of society's remaining major taboos, is of such limited incidence as to be almost insignificant.

Stroking a dog or cat is sensual. It is not intellectual, moral or sexual. It is physical. It is the gratification of the senses of touching and seeing. It is relaxing. It lowers the blood pressure as we have already seen. The sensuality in the relationship between people and their pets is related to the colour and texture of the animal's coat, to the song and plumage of the bird, and to the shape and movement of the pet in action or at rest.

Look at a real, live, honest-to-goodness, sleeping kitten. Concentrate only on that. Look at its colour, at the way it has shaped its body. Watch the slight movement of the hair over its chest as its heart beats, and observe how it breathes. That relationship between people and their pets is a sensual one and it is an aspect of the intimacy we have with them.

We are intimate with them in other ways too. My guess is that the majority of my patients sleep with their owners, and that many of them sleep in the same bed. Actually, it's not a guess, it's a fact. I did a survey in my practice and asked each pet owner where their pet slept. The results are as follows:

	DOGS	CATS
In Bedroom	52%	50%
In Own Bed	26%	15%
In Owner's Bed	26%	35%

As you can see, the majority of owners sleep with their pets. I didn't ask them, but I suspect that none of those who have children allow their children to sleep with them. Not only do owners sleep with their pets, but their sleeping patterns become the same. The electric changes in the brain, the electroencephalograph pattern in both the owner and the pet can become synchronous or harmonious.

Intimacy is shown in the way we play with pets. It is the same as the way we play with children. The point of a game is to play the game, not to establish a winner. I provoke my dog to play (or she provokes me to play, depending on who

The majority of owners sleep with their pets

is in the mood) simply to play. The children might join in to prolong the play, or may well have started it in the first place, but it is all open-ended. The game ends when one side or the other tires.

If a dog is small enough, we carry it in an intimate way. I see people pull dogs and cats out of the most incredible places. James Thurber has dubbed this carriage of dogs "pomeranianism". This type of intimacy need not be restricted to dogs and cats. I recall having a meal one evening at the Royal Society of Medicine, with Oliphant Jackson, a veterinarian who has spent a good part of his working life in East Africa. Dinner was early, as we had a meeting to attend, but the restaurant was full. We talked about I know not what, and as dessert came, Oliphant gave a little shuffle to the left, and then to the right, and then to the left again. I was dying to ask what was happening, but he beat me to it.

Moving his tie aside and undoing one button, he reached in under his shirt and withdrew a ten-inch snake. "I'm keeping it warm," he said, "but it's just become a little active." And he popped it back in, did his button up and launched into his apple crumble.

Granted, there was more than intimacy involved. The snake had been unwell and Oliphant wanted to keep it warm. But it was his snake, and he considered it only normal that his own body heat was the best way of assuring the reptile the care it needed.

I don't know if Oliphant Jackson actually loved that snake, but love is about the most common emotion I see between owners and their animals. George Bernard Shaw said that animals "bear more than their natural burden of human love", and from a behavioural view he is probably correct. Many behavioural problems are caused by the owner's wish to love the pet. By far the most common dietary problem I see is malnutrition, not through neglect but as a result of a wish to show one's love for the animal. Many, many owners feed their dogs and cats rich, red meat diets. They feel they are returning the love that the animal gives them by doing the only thing they think their pets will appreciate; giving the pet what it wants. It's an unnatural diet and both calcium and B vitamin deficiencies inevitably develop.

Overfeeding is very often another manifestation of this excessive love. I see dogs and cats that are actually killed with kindness. They are overfed to the point where they are unable to cope with ailments that would not otherwise be fatal. Many owners have a guilt feeling about the great love their pets have for them, not the least of whom is Konrad Lorenz, the pre-eminent animal behaviourist, who said in his book *Understanding Dogs*, "The plain fact that my dog loves me more than I love him is undeniable and always fills me with a certain feeling of shame."

I have always found it strange that Lorenz, such a brilliant observer of animal behaviour, would describe his dog's attitude to him as "love". Perhaps it was a result of his decades of observations on the lifetime bonding in pairs of Greylag Geese, a fact as warm and as sentimental as one would ever hope to observe. The relationship is not simply love. Certainly, some dogs and cats become obsessively attached to one individual, but equal numbers are fickle in their relationships. Yes, I know. Lorenz was describing his dog and its "love" for him, but it is still anthropomorphizing to describe the relationship as "love".

The fact that it is anthropomorphizing is almost irrelevant, however, to the way we feel. What is important is the way pet owners feel about their pets, and most pet owners feel that they love their pets and that their pets reciprocate. This is an important point, because in personality tests pet lovers (that means people who have pets and like them, or who don't have pets but would like to) exhibit greater affiliative tendencies than non pet lovers. In other personality tests, pet owners score significantly higher in what are called "favourable adjective" scores, indicating responsibility, dependability and lack of egotism. They are also, incidentally, according to these personality tests, less houseproud.

I think it is safe to say that pet lovers are different from pet haters. That's not really saying very much because in a recent very thorough survey only 4% of people interviewed said they disliked dogs. Interestingly, 27% said they disliked cats, giving statistical proof to the publisher of the book *101 Uses For A Dead Cat* who said it would be offensive to produce a book called *101 Uses For A Dead Dog* and besides there was no market for it.

Roberta Beck says she hates her cat. In *Cat Catalog – The Ultimate Cat Book* she explains why:

1. *For getting his white hairs on my black pants and his black hairs on my white pants.*
2. *For chewing the edges off my best typing paper and, when that is done, for sliding off the mounds of paper as though he were in training for the Winter Olympics.*
3. *For preferring lamb and liver to fish and chicken.*
4. *For thinking my garbage is the leftovers of the Garden of Eden.*
5. *For terrorizing and exploiting my dog, Tubby.*
6. *For knowing my threats are empty ones.*

Judy Fireman, the editor of the book, added a footnote to the list. "Roberta Beck's cat is a lemon."

The vast majority of people do not dislike dogs or cats, but within that majority there is a substantial percentage who actively like or love and want them. Social change is one of the newer factors affecting this group. Let me give you an example.

Recently, I had to euthanize an old Siamese cat in the terminal stages of kidney failure. It had shrunk to skin and bone, was off its food and its kidney function tests were off the end of the scale. Its owner, a women in her fifties, grieved over its loss, but went out immediately and bought a new kitten. A few days after she acquired this new pet, it developed what proved to be a fatal viral infection called panleucopenia.

It died rapidly after the onset of clinical signs. I counselled the owner that the disease was very contagious and that it was best not to allow any other cats in her flat for at least a month, preferably three months. A week later she was back with another cat suffering from a terminal panleucopenia infection. "But why did you get another cat so soon?" I asked. "I can't help it," she replied, "I can't bear to be alone, even for one night. My husband died two years ago, my daughter has emigrated to Australia and my son has moved to Southampton." And she cried. And she told me that she had come to London from "up north" to find a job, lived alone, didn't know her neighbours and dreaded not having something alive with her. My nurses resolved the problem, initially with a temporary budgie and finally with a fully vaccinated cat, but this lady's problem was not unique.

In Britain today more than one person in ten lives alone. By the end of the decade it is estimated that one in eight will be living alone. This is perhaps one of the greatest social changes that has occurred since the Industrial Revolution. For countless generations, we have lived in socially stable communities, usually as three generation extended families. Yet in this century, with emigration and increased mobility, this has suddenly ceased. Again, I am only talking about western culture, but within this culture there has been a sudden and precipitous change in the influence of the family, of the community and of religion, and within this culture, because it has been acceptable to keep pets, and because they were there, pets have slipped into the void.

Social change encompasses more than that. As western culture became more urbanized and as the urban sector became more affluent, both increasing boredom and decreasing contact with nature set in. We have seen the effects of increased "leisure time', a good euphemism for boredom, manifest themselves in an increased interest in sports, for example. We all need a certain amount of stimulation to work properly, and play of any sort can provide this in the presence of boredom. We try and find distractions, and I see this most blatantly in pet owners who live in council flats, and in affluent "house-bound" businessmen's wives. Dogs and cats can become the natural Valium for these people. It gives them something to do, be it to buy rhinestone collars for them or to knit winter bootees.

The urbanization of western culture has intervened in the symbiotic relationship we have had with nature for millions of years. A few years ago, the BBC transmitted a marvellous Finnish film that really captured the anxieties that this has caused. Put simply, it was the story of a man from Helsinki, and his pet rabbit. The film followed this man's escape from Helsinki, to the north and into the woods. He slept with his rabbit, he talked to it, he commiserated, but when out of the city, his relationship was different. In the woods, he was in the rabbit's own territory and there the rabbit was supreme. The rabbit was taking him back to nature; was taking him back to his roots. Corny, isn't it? But true.

For millions of years we have lived in common with the rest of the natural world, and in those millions of years, we have evolved genetically to live in harmony with it. This harmony resulted in symbiosis; a relationship whereby each species helps each other, but each is able to survive separately. We evolved to live symbiotically with other animals. Almost every culture in the world keeps pets, although the degree of care will vary tremendously. In our culture, we have deemed that they should be humanely care for. It has fascinated me that certain cultures have had difficulties in doing otherwise. Take the Bedouin, for example. The Bedouin look upon the dog as being unclean. In the early 'seventies this conflict between Bedouin and dog was transported from the Arabian Peninsula to Hyde Park and Kensington Gardens.

In the summer of 1973, an undeclared war erupted in London. It was fought between the indigenous urban British dog and Arab tourists. I first heard of it when clients told me of their pets being chased by groups of Arab girls in the parks. Gradually, I heard more stories of dogs being hit with sticks, of stones being thrown at them and, in one case, of a pram filled with Mothercare shopping bags being pushed into a group of Kerry Blue Terrier pups. (In that instance, the pups' owner pushed the pram, with some considerable force, back into its pusher.) On one occasion, I had to treat a Beagle that suffered a partial paralysis as a result of a blow with a branch.

This was a cultural phenomenon. In their home culture the dog is an unclean animal, a carrier of rabies, and one avoids contamination. Arabs who have become anglicized through living in Britain will adopt a British cultural attitude towards dogs and cats and will kill them with kindness to the same degree as the natives. One Arab Palestinian client of mine has tears in his eyes each time he brings his dog in, be it for routine vaccination or because of actual disease. And each time I reassure him that his pet is well and healthy, he grasps my hand with both of his and shakes it until the screws come loose. Inevitably, the next day, my nurses and I are showered with gifts.

What one could call the "new Arabs", those who have come to London since 1973 and who have settled here, also emulate the cultural customs of the natives, but do so only superficially. I see Great Danes compressed into the back compartments of Lamborghinis, but they are kept for show, because we keep them. There is no real bond. In their home culture, the dog is still taboo.

But here comes the dichotomy. What is the breed with the longest pedigree? The Saluki. And who bred it? The Bedouin! Although the dog is an unclean animal by Arab custom, the Saluki is not. It has special dispensation, as it were, and is not sullied by being referred to as a breed of dog. It is simply a Saluki. Symbiosis wins out.

Notwithstanding society's increasing concern about the aesthetic mess created by dogs being allowed to pass their droppings anywhere, our culture is evolving a more sympathetic attitude towards animals. The most recent small manifestation of this has been Shropshire County Council's decision to instal escape ramps in all new cattle grids in order to enable hedgehogs to leave the depression under the grid if they fall through. Our attitude towards zoos is changing. The Victorian concept of a garden full of wild animals to observe in their cages has become that of a community of animals living as close to their natural lifestyles as it is possible to recreate, without causing pain or suffering to other animals, and serving to provide knowledge so that their brethren in the wild can be better understood and maintained. The interest in naturally-occurring systems, ecology, sometimes has an unfortunate effect on our attitudes towards our pets.

Some of my clients look upon their dogs and cats as "natural" animals who should be allowed to roam freely, eat and reproduce as their instincts dictate, independent of any control from their owners. I have several clients who keep pets specifically for that reason; so that they can give these animals the freedom to "return to nature". They may be acting with the best of intentions but they are wrong, because they forget that they are themselves a part of their pets ecosystem. The consequence can only be detrimental. I asked one woman, after her dog had been killed by a car, why she continued to permit her other dog to run loose. She is not alone in this, incidentally. A Pet Food Institute survey showed that over one half of the dog owners interviewed saw no problem in their dogs running loose. Her answer was "Because I love him so much. If he gets killed, at least he's had an interesting life." This woman has two children. I know she loves them too. And I know she doesn't allow them to put themselves at risk in traffic. She suffers from a misguided attitude towards what is natural for her dog. It's one thing to live a Thoreau-like pastoral idyll in the woods, away from all the influences of society and with your dog roaming freely, capturing its own prey and finding a mate. It's quite another to live just off the Kings Road, to feed your dog mince and brown bread, and to have over 50,000 other dogs and cats living within a five mile radius. The dog and the cat are our creations. As such, we have taken on a responsibility for them. People who keep them so that they can "be free" only create greater problems for their pets and for their neighbours.

All in all, then, people keep pets today for a whole range of reasons. The old saw that they are child substitutes doesn't hold water. Most people say they get pets for their children. Aaron Katcher's and James Lynch's work seems to indicate that the bond between people and pets is different from the bond in human relationships; that it is neither a substitute for, nor a perversion of human relationships. Rather, it seems that the bond between people and pets supplements or augments what is available in human relationships.

It satisfies our need to nurture. But it does more. The bond between people and their pets is more controllable and less threatening than human relations. It can actually be warmer, and certainly less complicated. It can provide perfect speechless communication.

Being with your pet and just watching it or stroking it, or talking to it, can have a beneficial physiological effect on your body. It can reduce your blood pressure and lower anxiety. It may even help you to live longer.

Pets can certainly provide emotional security, and they can provide their owners with a feeling of constancy in a rapidly changing world. They can be a source of aesthetic pleasure and can relieve boredom by being a source of action and games, or a focus for pride. Most people think their pets understand their moods and in so doing share in their owners' ups and downs.

They can also bite, spread disease, get sick, destroy furniture, turn sidewalks into skidboards and bark louder than a Concorde on take off. Often, their disadvantages outweigh their advantages. The pros and cons of keeping pets are constantly changing. Our needs, as we grow and change, are always in flux. The roles that pets play are constantly changing, and that is what I shall discuss next.

CHAPTER FOUR

Pets and the family

I can't remember much about my family's first dog. He must have died when I was around five years old. Although we have home movies of him, my only memory of Angus, a Scottish Terrier, is of him wandering slowly down to the road, lying down by the curb, and eating the horse droppings left by the Brown's Bread and Silverwood Dairy wagons.

Our next dog, Sparkie, a large-boned Yorkshire Terrier, died in a road traffic accident when I was ten years old. I used to take this dog off to my room whenever I felt that the world was against me, and just sit and tickle her belly. She, of course, didn't mind. Her method of grasping my hand with her paws and bringing it down to her chest prolonged the exercise much beyond where it would have ended.

We had a cat at the same time. Both the cat and the dog had litter mates living next door, but then again so did my mother in a sense, as these animals belonged to her sister. Our cat, Blackie, disappeared on Friday, 13th June. The local baseball team, the Toronto Maple Leafs, offered free entrance to the stadium to anyone accompanied by a black cat. I wasn't too upset by its loss. I was always fonder of its sister next door. The death of Sparkie was a loss, however, I no longer had anything to tickle. We had tropical fish, painted turtles and six budgies, but none of these really meant anything to me.

When I was eleven, we got another Yorkshire Terrier, which we also named Sparkie. This was my closest pet. Although she was a family dog I always thought of her as mine. She was with me from public school until I left for

university. At university, my room-mates and I had various pets, a laboratory-bred Beagle, two scorpions, tropical fish, a grey tabby cat and a kinkajou; a fairly eclectic selection, but in retrospect probably only natural for a group of three veterinary students. Through it all, I still thought of Sparkie as my true pet, and friend.

Today, I have a Golden Retriever, Honey. She is terribly important because it is through her that I met by wife. She is a sweet old thing; the dog that is; not much of a sense of humour, but her very seriousness about life, and her warm affection, has bonded her firmly to us. She is fifteen now and will probably be unique amongst all the animals that have shared my home. She will probably be the most important pet I have had because without her my life would not have taken the course it has done.

All in all, I've lived with quite a few pets, but each one has served a different purpose. The role of each pet varied with both my age and my age-related needs, and with my other needs of companionship, of curiosity and of constancy. The same is true of my clients and their pets.

Pets play different roles and satisfy different needs in each family. As a veterinarian, the pet, to me, is a window to its family. The way it is treated, its name, the photos taken of it, the way it is groomed; all these things tell me something about the family. You might ask, why does a veterinarian need to know anything about the family? After all, he or she is there to treat the pet not the owners. The pet is not an isolated entity. It is usually the way it is for a whole wealth of reasons intermeshed into its relationship with the family. I want to know who acquired it and how, who does it belong to, and who is responsible for it, because all of these things will affect my diagnosis or advice or treatment.

The image of the typical, well-adjusted family today is that of a husband and wife, two to three children and a dog. The dog is very important to that image. It is so important that in 1980 all Republican candidates in the American general election were instructed to have themselves photographed with their pet dogs. That was probably very easy to do. A University of Pennsylvania survey revealed that all the owners who were asked, had photos of their dogs or cats.

Pets and the family

I am constantly being given photos of my patients. I have a desk full of pictures of red-eyed dogs and cats; pictures taken with a flash. They make an eerie selection. In most cases they are of the animal at play, but frequently they are of the cat or dog sitting or lying.

There is one elderly woman who I find I am compelled to see fairly regularly. Mrs Green is widowed and has lived for at least the last ten years alone, on the fourth floor of a building on the Lisson Grove Estate. She usually appears at the clinic unannounced, and after half an hour of chat, my receptionist usually sends her in to see me. Mrs Green is voluble but suffers the disability of forgetting the question she has just asked. That, naturally, means that my answers fall on her like water on a duck's back. There is something, however, that sharpens her memory and increases her alertness. During each visit she produces from her handbag large, individual colour photos of her eight living budgies. She also produces photos of two birds that died several years ago. She will, each visit, ask me, moist-eyed, why the birds died, and then go on to show me the pictures of the survivors. She will tell me when each picture was taken and why. Georgie, a blue budgie, had his picture taken on his first birthday. Stella.

The image of the typical well-adjusted family –
husband, wife, two to three children, dog

a green bird, had her taken on Mr and Mrs Green's wedding anniversary. Freddie's picture is very important because the photographer couldn't come to her flat to take it, and Mrs Green had to take Freddie to the photographer's in a taxi, a first experience for both of them. Ultimately, Mrs Green always goes back to four pictures she carries of her first bird, Ruby. They are all the same. She always gives me one, or tries to give me one, but always has four pictures in her handbag. She tells me that Ruby was the first bird she had after her husband died. Sometimes she shouts at me, asking why it died. Other times she asks if the others will catch the same illness. And finally, with some considerable difficulty, I manage to get Mrs Green to leave, usually with some vitamin impregnated birdseed or other such innocuous substance, so that she feels she is doing something for her birds.

Mrs Green and her photographs are, admittedly, a little bit of an unavoidable nuisance in practice, but they tell a lot about the significance of photographs of pets to their owners. The photo also tells a lot about the owner.

Most families look upon their family photo albums as important documents. They are frequently almost narratives of the lives of the family members, recording historically significant events and people. We photograph what we feel positive about. Most families tend to take more pictures of their first-born children, and of all of their children when they are young. Jay Ruby, who has studied the symbolic implications of animal photography, says that pictures of pets stylistically resemble pictures of babies and infants. Photographically, pets occupy the position of preverbal infants in family pictures.

Photographs or the actual act of taking a photo can serve a number of purposes. Mrs Green's pictures of her budgies aid her memory. They remind her of what she wanted to say. But they do other things as well. All her pictures have both a social and a historical importance. The actual taking of a picture was a social event, involving the presence of a photographer, and to Mrs Green a moment of excitement in an otherwise humdrum existence. But Mrs Green didn't choose to have pictures taken at random. She chose dates which were significant to her. One was a bird's birthday, another was her anniversary. Each picture has a historical significance in her life. Mrs Green's album of pictures of her birds is almost a Bible to her. In a sense it is her family bible. The images record important events and they elicit from her a candid, honest and emotional response that tells a great deal about her dependence on her pet birds. When Mrs Green gives me a picture of Ruby, she is sharing an emotion with me.

Mrs Green's story does not have a happy ending. I still see her at least once a month, and she still shows me pictures of all her birds, but they all died within fifteen minutes of one another almost six months ago. Through a fault in either her gas cooker or the heating in her flat, all of them asphyxiated. The only memory of her "family" is her collection of pictures. There is more anger now when she drops in, and more tears. But also more illness. Mrs Green has been in and out of hospital repeatedly since her birds died. She might have been a nuisance, but she was a vibrant nuisance. Her brood has died and she has nothing to live for.

Although less than half of my clients live in good old fashioned family units, that is, two-parent with child (or children) groups, I consider all of them to be members of families, even those living alone. I have a very broad definition of what a family is. If two individuals have a close attachment and share emotions or experiences and live together, I consider them to be members of a family group. The vast majority of pet owners, ninety-eight out of each hundred, say they talk to their pets. More than three out of four say they feel their animal is sensitive to their moods, and more than one in four actually confides in his or her pet.

By that definition, people who live alone with their pets, as well as gay couples and widowers, constitute families because of their interactions with their pets. A family is naturally not a static thing. My family has finished its time of expansion and, when my eldest leaves home, it will enter a period of contraction. Marriages will bring inclusions. Conflicts might bring exclusions. Through all the harmonies and conflicts, changes and rearrangements, the domestic pet remains the same. The pet can be a great source of conflict, but it remains a family member, a symbol of constancy.

Most people, 87% in a recent survey, say their pet is a family member. In the same survey, when asked "Who do you feel closest to in your family?", surprisingly, most people said their pet.

The role of the pet in the family is, generally speaking, that of a surrogate human. Eighty per cent of people talk to their pet "as a person" not "as an animal". Linguists at the University of Pennsylvania say that pet owners use a type of language they have dubbed "motherese" when they speak to their pets. Motherese is the language used by mothers when talking to infants and young children. Pets are treated as surrogate children. And most people, when asked why they got pets, answer "for the children".

I think that this answer is deceiving both the questioner and the respondent. My clients tell me that "my dog is my best friend" or that "she understands me more than my family does" or "I wish my children were as well behaved as he is". They give the expected answer "It's for the kids". But underneath it all, symbolically or otherwise, it is really for them.

In Britain today, the number of married couples with children is the same as the number without children. Paul McCutcheon, a veterinarian in Toronto, surveyed his practice and came up with more surprising figures. Only 31% of McCutcheon's clients were from classical family units. Over 24% were "empty nesters"; married couples whose children had left home. Almost as many, 23%, were single people living alone, and 18% were childless couples. The remaining 4% of his clients were single parent families.

In almost all surveys, pet ownership declines as level of education and income rises. This applies equally to London where, in the affluent north-west quadrant, 29% of households have pet dogs and cats, whereas in the poorer south-east quadrant, 51% of households have them, and to Newfoundland, surely the end of the canine/feline world, where similar observations have been made. But everywhere, the answer is the same; "We got the dog/cat for the children." Let's follow through the significance of a pet to one individual from infancy to old age.

Babies don't need pets. They can do no good. In fact, infants and crawlers should be protected from the affectionate excesses of dogs and cats. The parents are another story. Bernard Rollins, an escapee from New York City, who teaches philosophy at Colorado State University, says, "You can only talk to other people in New York if you have a baby or a dog!" The advantages won't be so clear to the baby until he has reached Rollins's age. Meanwhile, as far as I am concerned, pets offer nothing to the infant, other than possible harm. For the first six months of life, a child, from our present understanding, is unaware of anything outside of, or different from, itself, and even when it does recognize this difference, the distinction between animate and inanimate objects is not yet developed. If you are getting a pet, and wish to introduce it to an infant, or if you have a pet and want to introduce it to the new baby, there are rules you simply must follow.

Dogs and cats are curious and should not be disciplined for their curiosity. Allow them to see and smell the baby when the baby is sleeping. If you can, combine that experience with something that is pleasurable to the animal, like giving it a treat or stroking it. A dog that has been number one in a

Infants and crawlers should be protected from the affectionate excesses of dogs and cats

household will feel usurped if a baby is brought into the home and attracts all the attention. The dog should have its own special time for activity each day. Play with the animal to let it know that its position in the household hierarchy has not been changed.

My experience is that it is very unwise to isolate the dog from the baby. It only increases the dog's curiosity and heightens the risk of an accident. Finally, never leave the baby and dog alone together. Most people simply forget that their dog is a dog. If you live with one for a while, you begin to think that it is just a human that has gone slightly wrong. Parents of babies should think of their dogs as wolves, even if the dog only weighs five pounds, until they are satisfied that their child can defend him or herself.

Studies in New York State show that pets can elicit maternal behaviour in children as young as three-and-a-half years, and it is only at this age that I can see benefits in the relationship. That is not to say that younger children should not have pets, but rather that children must be this old to treat the pets reasonably well and to take advantage of what the pet has to offer. Pets can become fun now for both the child and the parent. The active pet is fun to follow around, and can help the child to develop motor skills. It is also probably more tireless than the mother and father, and can actually take some of the responsibility for playing with the child.

Parents of babies should think of their dogs as wolves until they are satisfied that their child can defend him or herself

74

Jim Van Leeuwen, a psychiatrist at the Hospital for Sick Children in Toronto, has written that pets can provide children with experience of reality, with stimulation and with play. Ange Condoret, a veterinarian in the South of France, has made an exceptional study of the role of pet animals in a local kindergarten class. Condoret recorded on

. . . more tireless than the mother and father,
and can actually take some of the responsibility for
playing with the child

videotape the interactions between the children in the class and a resident dog and cat. He calls the experience "live pedagogy". He says that the spontaneity and freedom they introduced improved class integration as well as improving unsatisfactory relationships between children and their peers or teachers. This is very important because children form the basis of their future relationships between the ages of four and six years. Condoret says that the pet serves as a useful model for the children in forming positive relationships. On videotape, he has recorded how contact is made initially by touch. Touch leads to stroking and petting. As we have seen previously, this forms an attachment. Talking with the pets follows, and as most children feel that pets understand what they are saying, as do most adults as well, this discourse leads to true communication, which is a vital part of the socialization process. Condoret has a valid point. Studies of parents who abuse their children show that most had what are called negative relationships in childhood; that they lacked friends, hadn't had the "mothering imprint" and didn't have pets. In other words, these people had never formed positive relationships with people or pets and never had maternal behaviour elicited in them.

Pets are usually introduced into families that already have children, and most pets live in families with children, a fact that would indicate that animals complement the companionship offered by children, rather than substitute for it. Aaron Katcher hypothesizes that parents buy pets after their children are beyond the cuddling stage. My clients seem to have them already when they get married, and buy pets when their existing ones die. Katcher, however, says that in his surveys a dog is usually introduced to the urban child after it has had considerable experience with stuffed toys. Although he doesn't like the use of the term in this context, because he thinks it suggests too narrow a role, the dog is essentially a transitional object; a direct descendant from the mother's breast, the satin-edged blanket, the soft toy and the stuffed animal. All of these things allow the child to feel safe and active, and engaged without the presence of, or interaction with, the parents. A child needs to love and be loved. A child needs warmth and security. But the child also needs to use its imagination, to daydream, to live in its own world. Children have to distance themselves from their parents and the younger they are the more difficult it is to do. The presence of a pet might make it easier.

Ten years is the minimum age when a child can reasonably care for a pet. In younger children, almost 70% of their dreams involve animals and up to the age of seven years of these dreams are fearful, involving animal attacks. This would have given the child a survival advantage in primitive society. Today it only gives nightmares. After that age, fearful animal dreams diminish but still occur. Noisy dogs with dark coats seem to induce more fear in children than do others. But by the age of ten years, the dog can offer an array of benefits.

Boris Levinson, a psychiatrist at Yeshiva University, has written two books on the subject of pets and childhood development. He says that to children pets can act as confidants, offer emotional support, be a source of continuity

A dog is usually introduced to the urban child after it has had considerable experience with stuffed toys

under stress and facilitate learning in relation to friendliness, toilet training, sex behaviour, pregnancy and death. A survey in Scotland, of parents of children with pets, showed that 50% of them felt similar to Levinson. George Papashvily has quoted this story written by an eight-year-old named John Morrison in 1947 in Rochester, New York.

"My dog means somebody nice and quiet to be with. He does not say 'Do' like my mother, or 'Don't' like my father, or 'Stop!' like my brother. My dog, Spot, and I sit together quietly and I like him and he likes me. The end."

Children almost invariably think of their pets as members of the family. A teacher in a New York parochial school presented this situation to her ten-to-twelve-year-old pupils. "You are picnicking at the shore of a lake. Suddenly, you hear a commotion and see people pointing to your dog and a strange man, who are both drowning some distance from the shore. You're a good swimmer, but you know you can only save one. Which one would you save?"

Most of the students said they would save the dog and 90% of these were from pet-owning homes. The students gave reasons such as "The pet is a member of my family", or "He protects me and I must protect him".

Children at this age have strong "family" needs. I know of many families who have pets to alleviate the "lack of family" for the children because both parents work. Alasdair Mac-Donald, a psychiatrist, has recounted a case to me involving a single parent family in which the children were left at home alone with the dog. After the dog died the children became very distressed when they were left at home, but the situation was readily alleviated when a new pup was brought in. The pup, in effect, became the surrogate parent.

Children, however, are the part of the community at greatest risk from dogs. I don't mean from the transmission of roundworm larva; a topic that has become an overblown, melodramatic issue, and is of minor significance compared to some of the more serious problems that children can face. I mean dog bites.

I shall say more about dog bites in chapter 6, but because of the danger they represent within the family context, I must make some mention of the problem here. The Hospital for

Sick Children in Toronto sees as much physical damage done to children through dog bites as it sees injuries caused by child abuse. Children are bitten by dogs more frequently than are adults, and although adults are usually bitten on the arms and legs, over 75% of children's bites are on their heads. Blaming the child for the bite simply isn't valid. It harkens back to the time when the rape victim was blamed rather than the rapist. Dogs usually bite on their home territory, or very near to it, and 70% of reported bites are done by males. The children most at risk are those between seven and ten years of age; and bites occur more frequently in summer than in winter; in sunshine rather than in rain.

In almost all surveys, the Alsatian is near the top of the list in offenders. This mirrors the fact that in actual numbers it is one of the most numerous breeds, but also indicates that it is one of the most poorly managed breeds. The Canadian Medical Association has gone on record saying, "that the public be cautioned against the keeping of large dogs, especially the Alsatian." One in every one hundred children will be bitten by a dog before the age of ten, and when you consider that an Alsatian's jaws have a crushing power of 150–200 pounds per square inch, it doesn't take much imagination to see what type of damage can be done.

It is not easy for the veterinarian to decide whether there has been negligence on the part of the parents, and what to do if he thinks there has been. Let me give you a true case, although I have changed the owners' names in this instance.

Wendy and Marty Fine were a couple, married for ten years, with two sons aged four and six. They had a good income and lived in an affluent part of London. They had had a Weimaraner since their first child was born, but decided to get another dog, and chose a German Short Hair Pointer. I had known the family for six years on a first name basis.

When they brought the pup in at twelve weeks of age for its vaccination, it was obvious that the dog had dominant characteristics. It showed true aggression rather than playfulness, although at that age it simply seemed cute to the owners. I told Wendy and Marty that the dog would prove to be difficult, and suggested that they attend professional dog obedience classes.

I didn't have cause to see the dog until it was returned at fifteen months of age for its booster vaccination. It pulled Wendy into the examining room, sniffed around, cocked its leg on my desk, took a sniff at my crotch, almost lifting me to the ceiling in the process, and proceeded to drag Wendy back out of the room.

I grabbed the lead, brought the dog back in, examined it, vaccinated it, and asked Wendy "how things were going". She told me the dog was a handful. It wouldn't stay in the garden and roamed the neighbourhood mating everything, animal, vegetable or mineral, it could mount.

As she was leaving, she said, "By the way. You were right. He's tried to bite Jason twice." I asked a nurse to look after the dog and I sat down and discussed with Wendy what had happened. She told me that, for no apparent reason, the dog has snapped at Jason, the four-year-old, twice, on both

It pulled Wendy into the examination room

occasions leaving tooth impressions and a bruised face but not drawing blood.

This is a situation that every practising veterinarian has been in, and I offered Wendy three alternatives. After explaining that it was sheer luck that more serious damage had not been done, I told her that I would find the dog a new home, or I would euthanize it, or I would arrange for behaviour modification training in conjunction with castration. I told her I would keep the dog at the Clinic while she discussed everything with her husband, but she said it was her husband's dog and she would have to take it home.

Two days went past, and having heard nothing from them, I telephoned Marty at work. He said, yes, Wendy had told him what I had said, but when I asked him what he wanted me to do, he said, "Listen, Bruce, I like that dog just the way he is. You can cut yours off, but you're not touching my dog's!"

And that was it. For whatever the reasons were, he liked that dog the way it was. I don't know whether he didn't like his younger son, or whether the dog was a manifestation of the freedom that he wished he had, but I never saw him again.

Six months later I returned in August from a visit to Canada, to hear from a colleague of mine that he had killed the dog at the owner's request. It had once more gone for the little boy's head, but this time tore off his scalp. Jason has just had his third skin transplant from his hip to his head, and is scarred physically and mentally for life.

Pets can be great fun for children, but until the child is old enough to carry the responsibility of caring for the animal, it is the parent or owner's responsibility to do the following:

1. Children should be taught never to approach strange animals.
2. Children should be taught to respect animals and to be aware of danger signals and how to react to them.
3. Children should be taught never to put their faces close to an animal's face or claws.
4. Children should be taught to be wary of dogs raised in homes in which there are no children.

Small children should never exercise large dogs

5. Children should be taught that a dog will protect its home and to be careful when entering a house with a dog.
6. Children should be taught never to try to stop two dogs fighting, even if one is their own.
7. Children should be taught never to disturb an eating or sleeping animal.
8. Children should be taught never to carry food near an animal.
9. Children should be supervised when they meet new animals.
10. Children should be supervised when they are learning to feed their pet.
11. Children should be supervised when they are learning to exercise their pet.
12. Small children should never exercise large dogs.

Adolescence brings with it a changing relationship to pets. The dog I had as an adolescent, Sparkie the second, was the dog I was most attached to. Looking back now, I was attached because, for the first time, there was responsibility on my part. I liked looking after it. When Mary Stewart, a veterinarian on the faculty of the University of Glasgow, arranged for comprehensive school students to write essays on why they liked their pets, 41% liked them most because of the responsibility that was entailed in looking after them. The character of the pet, and the fun of playing with it, were the other important factors.

Character is difficult to define. The students used words like happy, cheerful, kind, loving, faithful, gentle, intelligent and appealing to describe their pets character. All of these terms are anthropomorphic. They give human attributes to the pet and are mostly a result of our interpretation of the pet's facial expression, and of the position of its ears and tail.

James Serpell, at Cambridge University, looked into this further. Knowing that both facial expression and the gaze pattern were important in initiating communication between people, Serpell wanted to investigate people's responses to dogs' faces and bodies in photographs. He prepared black and white pictures of the Old English Sheepdog, Labrador, English Setter, Corgi and Dachshund. Each dog was photographed head on, in profile and obliquely, both in close-up of the head and at a distance, photographing the entire body. He then showed the pictures to various groups of children and adults. What he observed was that all groups preferred pictures of large dogs and, generally speaking, all preferred close-ups of the head. The one exception was the Old English Sheepdog. Most people preferred full body pictures of that breed.

Serpell's results were consistent with the observation that we pick up signals and define an animal's character from its facial expression. The Old English Sheepdog is an anomaly, probably because it is so widely used in advertising that its whole body signals, quite apart from the fact that you can't see its eyes in the first place.

Adolescence can bring a few problems for the pet as well, for this is the age group that is most likely to torment pets. The cats that I see that have been shot with air rifles or set on fire are always the victims of teenagers.

Because animals are subordinate, they are always vulnerable to redirected aggression. This is their fate, regardless of the age of the owner, but where adolescents are concerned there is the additional torment that comes from the process of experimenting.

Animals are treated cruelly, even sadistically, by children in most primitive societies. Australian Aborigines keep tame wallabies, possums, bandicoots and cassowaries in their camps. The Inuit of northern Canada adopt bear cubs, foxes, birds and baby seals. South American jungle tribes will keep agoutis, pacas, parrots, boa constrictors and capuchin monkeys as pets. All share in the same neglect and maltreatment of these animals, and they are either killed or allowed to die

. . . wanted to investigate peoples responses to dogs' faces and bodies . . .

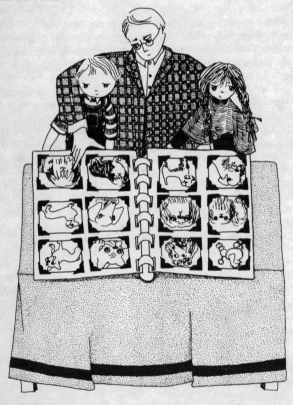

when their amusement value declines.

Wild animals may well, at one time, have had value as pets because hunters could learn to understand their nature, and therefore be better at hunting them. And the sadistic behaviour to which pets are subjected in these societies could be part of their cultural training to prepare them to be dominant and aggressive towards animals; traits that would serve them well when they became adult hunters. In certain pastoral societies, redirected hostility towards pet animals could be an important part of a restricted emotional repertoire.

I am pleased to say, however, that most psychiatrists believe that minor ill-treatment of animals is a developmental stage we go through. I am pleased to say it because I used to take my cat, Blackie, up to the top of the stairs, cradle her on her back through the bannister, and drop her. I wanted to see if she really would roll over in the air and land on her feet. At the same age, I used to give frogs injections with pine needles and, I'm afraid to say, tie them to stumps in "frog bog" and wait all day for a water snake to come along and eat them whole.

Tormenting is a stage, but it can persist in boys who need to display dominance. Persistent or recurrent cruelty to animals predicts a future of violence, however. When one researcher examined one hundred adults who had made threats to kill others, he found frequent childhood occurrence in these people of bedwetting, fire setting and cruelty to animals.

The adolescent leaves home and very often, for the first time in his or her life, has complete independence. In London, many of these people, especially the women, quickly acquire pets. One in every four of Paul McCutcheon's clients in his practice in Toronto was a single person living alone. I would guess that the figure is probably the same in my practice.

The pet can take on totally new significance at this age. It can be a confidant, an object of love, a protector, a social facilitator, a teacher, a sex object or a status symbol. Creating an identity is very important at this age and the use of pets to do that is very common. Ten years ago it seemed that every frosted blonde model I saw had a frosted blonde Afghan by her side. They looked exquisite walking in Hyde Park and Kensington Gardens, and made terrible bad debts.

Pets have always been used as symbols of status, or class or power in stratified societies. People who have achieved, or aspire to achieve, higher status acquire pets that allow them to participate in the sports of the upper classes. Two hundred years ago, they advertised their possessions by having George Stubbs and his contemporaries paint portraits of them. Pets are still today animated symbols of group identity. A working Springer Spaniel or Labrador Retriever is as much a symbol as the Hermes scarf or Gucci belt. The Afghan, certainly one of the most graceful breeds of dog, is the perfect compliment to the woman who wants to project a racy, windswept image. Her choice is an act of self definition, as important as her hair style or clothing.

Young heterosexual men, if they get pets, almost invariably get large dogs, usually of the short-haired breeds. Young homosexual men, on the other hand, will frequently have cats or small dogs, as well as long and short-haired large

Every frosted blonde model had a frosted blonde Afghan by her side

breeds. Homosexual women will, in London at least, have the same variety of pets as their male counterparts.

I should indicate a professional prejudice here. I find the pet owning male homosexual clients to be probably the most concerned, responsible and responsive of any group that I see. They bring their pets in at the first sign of trouble, follow instructions carefully and are exceptionally grateful for successful treatment. That is not to say that they can't be tricky if things aren't going well, but generally speaking they are among the most pleasing of groups of pet owners.

A pet, to a homosexual couple, is very often an expression of that couple's identity as a discrete family unit. The shared responsibility of pet ownership reinforces in the owners the feeling of living in a family unit. In my experience, homosexual couples will do more, and put up with more, to keep the family unit intact than will heterosexual couples.

Jim Wright and Timothy Hunt have a male Great Dane that I have treated since it was a pup. Wright and Hunt live on the third floor of a Georgian terrace house in Islington, and their dog, Sam, is now ten years old. Two years ago, Sam developed the first signs of a spinal cord disease which is progressive and incurable. The nerves in the spinal cord lose their protective sheathing, and when this happens the nerves become useless. The first sign was simply knuckling over of the hind paws, but over the months and years, as the disease progressed up the spinal cord towards the front, the dog lost control of its bladder and most control of its hind legs. Can you imagine the problems involved in having an incontinent Great Dane in a third floor flat? It must be as if the roof had been leaking for eighteen months.

Wright and Hunt, however, learned how to catheterize and empty the bladder, how to treat bedsores when they, most fortunately infrequently, occurred, how to support the dog when it tried to get up and then how to assist gently while it walked around. It could even run, and enjoyed the exercise when they lightly supported a band under its belly. I didn't suggest killing the dog when it developed this disease, a suggestion I might have made under different circumstances, because I knew that Sam would get twenty-four-hour nursing and as much loving care as the most dearly loved child. I also knew that, by the very nature of the disease, there would be no pain, as the actual conductors of pain sensation were being destroyed. And as for the breed, well, the Great Dane is the most laid back breed going. They probably need less exercise than most other breeds, and prefer to live their lives in a semi-cataleptic state, opening their eyes rather infrequently to see if a new day has dawned. A colleague, Nicholas Larkins, recently invited me to a wedding reception which his wife's mother was having for the couple. When I, and around five hundred other guests, met Nicholas and Miranda, at Miranda's home, I noticed their Great Dane sound asleep on the sofa. We ate, we drank, we danced, we went home. I imagine the Dane woke up the next day. It certainly didn't while we were there. Danes are not party goers in the way that terriers are.

Pet ownership is higher amongst young people, homosexual or heterosexual, who have formed permanent relationships. Students at the University of Pennsylvania who are unattached only infrequently have pets, while students who either live together, or who are actually married, have a much higher level of pet ownership. They probably do so because the parenting involved in mutually caring for a cat or dog fulfils the psychological need for a child where in practice it is impractical to have "the real thing". Young couples today frequently postpone having their own families for a number of years. Both may be working. They might be trying to build up a money reserve. They might want five to ten years of freedom to go where they want, when they want. But almost invariably, the pet is "ours". It is rarely "mine", or "his" or "hers". The nesting instinct is mutual. When children arrive, the pets don't necessarily take a back seat, but the parents don't have as great a personal need to interact with the pet. Sharon Smith, at the University of Pennsylvania, has made some interesting observations on how childless couples and families with children interact with their pets. She observed that, in childless families, the people and the pet interacted more frequently, more readily and with more complexity.

Dr Smith's first observation was that, regardless of the presence or absence of children, pet dogs regularly monitored the availability of human contact. They either stayed in the same room as their owners, or perhaps one room away. In childless families, the dogs spent relatively more time within three feet of the owner than in families with children. Childless couples would frequently interrupt what they were doing to talk to or touch their pets, and would, on average, do so more than five times per hour. Couples with children seldom interrupted what they were doing, and on average interacted with their pets only once or twice an hour. This was the same, regardless of whether the children were present or not. Smith observed that men and women acted similarly in their response to their pets. Men who were away from home for longer periods than their wives, however, touched their pets at least twice as much as their wives did. All of this hand contact, of course, reinforces the attachment that you have for your pet.

Most parents think that a child will learn about responsibility and friendship, and learn to love and respect animals, by having pets. It is a belief mirrored in almost every primary school, a belief that pets are "good for children".

In practice, however, the pet very often serves the parent. It can act as a substitute for types of attachment that, for one reason or another, are not available in the marriage. Pets, for example, can satisfy the need for physical contact, if that type of attachment is not available elsewhere. In the same way, verbal, or even physical, abuse may be aimed at the pet as a means of attacking the partner on an emotional level, or as an expression of the violence that one would really like to inflict upon the other.

Remarriage is a normal event today, and countless psychologists have written unending books and articles on how the children of the failed marriage should be treated so that they are traumatized as little as possible. I don't think anyone, however, has written about what to do with the family pet. I'll discuss psychosomatic disease in dogs and cats further on, but let me give you an example of the type of problem that can occur in a marriage in which one of the partners already has a pet.

Clare married Raymond several years ago. Clare had lived independently for many years and, during that time, had acquired a miniature white poodle named Button. As with the majority of pets, Button always slept in Clares' bedroom. Shortly after they married they brought the dog in one day and Raymond took me to one side. "Listen, I have a problem. Each time I try to make love to my wife, I have a barking, biting Button on my back. Do you have a little something I can slip it in the evening? If I try to lock it out of the room, Clare will have nothing to do with me!"

Well, what do you do? Pets in marriage can be a real nuisance. My guess is that there is more trouble afoot than meets the eye. When one person recently told me that her husband was complaining about their Bull Terrier pup crawling between them at night, she said "That's all right. He can sleep somewhere else if he likes. The puppy stays where it is!"

As the children mature, the parents' relationship to the pets also changes. Some might say it regresses. Many parents now look to their pets for the affection and adoration they no longer receive from their children. This is the time when pets are more likely to be indulged or spoiled. The breed of dog doesn't make any difference here. Roger Mugford, a psychologist/ethologist who specializes in treating animal behaviour problems in London, sees little difference in the "parent giving" to various breeds, regardless of size.

The parents are reaching a major juncture in their lives. One by one their children leave home. What has been routine for twenty to thirty years is no longer necessary. All the activities, the comings and goings, no longer take place. In many instances, however, there is something to provide continuity. It is usually rather hairy, perhaps getting on a bit in years, but still willing to carry on as if little has changed. This may well be the time the pet plays its most important role in the lives of its owners. It may be indulged. It might not like its new knitted pullover. It might be taken for more walks or listen to longer monologues. It might take on more responsibility in guarding the house, or it might simply be there, as Thoreau put it, "stirring the dead air in the room". The nest is empty but the need to nurture remains.

Leo Bustad showed a slide at the beginning of a talk he gave to a group of doctors and veterinarians; the type of slide that American lecturers always use to get the attention of the audience. To the left of the picture was the tailend of a parked

It might not like its new knitted pullover

car. In the middle and to the right was Leo, dressed in running shoes and wind breaker holding his rather scrawny and, I think, toothless old dog in a running position. He said the caption to this slide was "My dog is sixteen but she still likes to chase cars". The real caption should have been "I'm sixty-five and both my dog and I would like to chase cars." Science can't cope with that, however, because it has set up different disciplines to study Leo and his dog.

Science has always compartmentalized. Endocrinologists study hormones and their function and dysfunction in the body. But they don't study that body's consequent actions in society because of those hormones. That is left to another science. The individual disciplines do not frequently meet and meld. And that is why it is interesting to look at disparate sciences' conclusions on the same subject.

Anthropologists study the behaviour of the human animal. Although they have a propensity for studying remote tribes in remote countries, they have the academic wherewithal equally to study social classes in our society, or pet owners for that matter. One of the things that the anthropologist is interested in is "What are the factors within a certain group which lead to best functioning and most contentment?" And they come up with the following. In Australian Aborigines or African Pygmies; in Amazonia Indians and Afghan herdsmen:

(a) a constant level of activity;
(b) good physical well-being;
(c) good relations with other members of the group;
(d) use of their skills;

are the four factors which most affect contentment.

Gerontologists study the aged and ageing, and they ask a similar question. They ask, "What are the main predictors of happiness in old age?" And the answers they come up with are

(a) having a spouse with whom you are relaxed and in whom you can confide;
(b) your spouse's good health;
(c) your physical activity;
(d) your self-rated health.

If you look at these results the anthropologists and geron-tologists have come up with a number of similar results. Whether you are a seventy-year-old white man in Florida or a thirty-year-old Indian in the Peruvian Andes, the most important factors that lead to happiness and contentment are physical activity and good relations with your spouse or with other members of your group.

Closer to home, the American National Institute of Health has looked into what factors are related to longevity. The most important factor is the best known. Don't smoke and you're guaranteed to live longer. But on the social side, having a complex, varied and interesting daily activity was found to be the strongest social predictor of longevity. Perhaps that is why symphony orchestra conductors live so long.

But what about the empty nesters? Their children have left home. Their daily activity suddenly becomes less varied, less interesting and less complex. When these people get new pets, they aren't just replacing their children. They are replacing the activity, the schedule of comings and goings. Besides seeing this in my practice, I can see it in my parents' home. "Well, Bejo," my father will say at 8.30 a.m., 12.30, 4.30, 9.00 and 11.00 p.m., "it's time to take you for a walk." Clockwork activity. "Come on, Bejo," my mother will say at 10.00 a.m. and 2.00 p.m., "I'm going for a walk."

Bejo has just entered their lives, a mutt of totally mixed-up ancestry, who seems part fox, part antelope, rescued by my sister from the deserts of Dubai and air-freighted to my parents. Bejo is not what anyone would call a beautiful dog. She's rather indescribable. But she has firmly imprinted herself on both of my parents and is providing them with what they need; responsiblity, devotion, security, activity, a talking point and a new source of play and exercise.

My father is semi-retired. He had his own business and my brother now runs it. The consequence of that is that he did not suffer the losses that can go with retirement. Retirement to some means loss of colleagues, status, money, house and often apparent purpose in life, as well as the job. A married couple can find themselves together in each other's company all day long for the first time in their lives. One man I know drops in at the clinic almost weekly to say hello and to tell me how lucky he is to have his dog. "She's a sweet 'gel'" he tells me, referring to his wife, "but I wouldn't wish living with her twenty-four hours a day on my enemies." Taking his dog for a walk is his way of relieving the domestic tension that has built up since he has retired and been at home.

Age groups are difficult to define. I see people who are old at thirty-five and young at seventy-five. Samuel Corson has studied the use of pets in therapy for the elderly as well as the stresses of compulsory retirement. He says, "Forced retirement at sixty-five or seventy of an individual in good physical, intellectual and emotional health may lead to a general deterioration, unless the individual can engage in some new, meaningful, satisfying activities." The French philosopher, André Maurois, once quipped: "Growing old is no more than a bad habit which a *busy* man has no time to form."

Dorothy Walster, who works with the Scottish Health Education Unit, has written several papers on the role of pets in the lives of the elderly. In one survey she conducted on people over sixty-five years of age, the most frequently mentioned benefits of pet ownership were "gives you something to do" and "gives you something to talk about". Cost was the biggest worry to the owners, although older owners spend more on their pets than any other group of pet owners.

The human is a social animal. We need to play a social role; to be useful and needed in order to maintain morale and self-esteem. Corson has observed that, in the absence of human sources, pets can provide elderly people with this role.

For all this, there can be no doubt that pets are still able to fulfil for the elderly one of our most basic needs, felt more perhaps in old age than at any other time – the need to nurture. Infants love to be stroked and petted, and parents enjoy the stroking. The feeling of holding a baby is something mothers never forget, and grandmothers yearn for. Most parents experience a comforting reverie when holding a relaxed baby. It's soothing and peaceful, and can lull the parent to sleep as well as the baby. My youngest daughter is my most sensuous child. She is also the trickiest, but I'd be quite happy to sit in a rocking chair, with her clasped onto me like a tree frog, arms around my neck and legs around my waist, head on my shoulder and hair in my face, until the cows come home.

Children grow up. They outgrow the clinging stage. But dogs don't. In fact, they are bred and trained specifically to be petted and not to reject it. Breeds have been anthropomorphized to have large heads and small bodies, and to have prominent eyes. The typical Pekingese looks as though it was really created as a Mabel Lucy Attwell drawing, with its lack of prominent features, its roundness, large eyes and constant activity. It even stops "crying" when you pick it up. And it is breeds of this sort which are most popular among the elderly people I see.

Loneliness is often cited as the worst aspect of ageing. The role of pets can then be obvious, but sometimes things get out of control. Until three years ago, when she died, I used to make monthly visits to a large, empty, redbrick, Victorian house in Hampstead to visit Miss Hibbert, a nursing sister during the Boer War in South Africa, retired to a basement room in what was her family's rather splendid home.

When we first met, her arthritis had not progressed to the point where she could no longer play the piano, and her hearing, although impaired, was still good enough to hear what I was shouting. While I ministered to her two cocker spaniels and fifteen to twenty feral cats, she told me stories of the first electric lights in Hampstead, the first motor car, life in the hospitals at the turn of the century and countless other stories of fascination. Over the next few years, her arthritis went on a rampage and her hearing disappeared. The district nurse visited twice weekly to give her a sponge bath, and her doctor visited frequently, both of them trying to convince her to move into a home where she could be given twenty-four hour care. She refused to go. She refused to go because of worry over her dogs and cats. I offered to look after the dogs. I had, in fact, hospitalized them on occasion when they needed anaesthesia or daily treatments that I knew she would be unable to give, but she refused to go because of the cats.

These cats were feral; wild; impossible for me to get anywhere near. Half a dozen would be sitting on her bed

when I would come into her room, but like bed bugs when a light is turned on, they were out of the window in a flash. "My kitties need me," she would tell me. Kitties? They were tigers who would have delighted in tearing me apart. "I can't leave my kitties." She did finally. But it was neither her choice nor her doctor's.

In the psychiatry of old age, senile dementia is probably the biggest problem. Although individuals have good recall of the past, their immediate memory is rather poor. Dorothy Walster recounts the use of a cat in one instance to help an elderly person to remember to do things. A local health board district in Scotland, in trying to combat the risk to the elderly of suffering from the cold in the winter, gave to all the elderly people at risk in the district simple, easy-to-read thermometers with a coloured band for readings below 60°F. One lady who persistently forgot to use her thermometer and neglected to keep her room heated was finally given a budgerigar. Almost immediately things changed, and to this day she and her budgie are living together comfortably at recommended room temperature.

Budgies make ideal pets for the elderly and, in fact, were used in the first study on the effects of pets on old people living alone. In 1974, Roger Mugford made a study of a city in the north of England. He divided a group of old people living alone into three groups. One group got a visit from a social worker, and a begonia plant. One group got a visit from a social worker, and a budgie. And one group simply got the visit from the social worker.

The social adjustment and mental health of these people were observed for the next five months through regular visits from the social worker, and through an extensive questionnaire. The results were enlightening. Those who had been given budgies showed significant improvements in a whole range of social attitudes, including self-esteem, mental health and all-round happiness. These people stopped talking primarily of their aches and pains, or impending demise, and talked instead about their birds. Mugford called the budgies "social lubricants", a rather oily description for such clean creatures.

Pets can provide the elderly with a link with the past, in that it is very often the case that the urban elderly of today grew up in a rural community and moved to the city to get jobs. A pet is a link to that earlier more natural world. The

. . . the use of a cat helps an elderly person to remember to do things

poet, May Sarton, put it more symbolically. She described the presence of a pet inside a house as a kind of wildness within, a counterpoint to the balance and order of culture.

The elderly are the fastest-growing segment of the community, and perhaps the least cared for. The World Health Organization reports that today the elderly in poorer, underdeveloped countries, live relatively better and enjoy a higher social status than in the richer, industrialized societies. It seems a shame to me that in our culture we leave them with dogs, cats and budgies to provide them with companionship, security and activity. Pets are fine, but should augment rather than supplant the care and attention that other humans should give.

Those who had been given budgies showed significant improvement

CHAPTER FIVE

Bereavement

Dogs and cats have shorter life expectations than their owners and this creates the greatest emotional problem we face in our relationship with them. The ultimate death of the pet and the remorse and grieving that it brings is the most often cited reason for not wanting another one. Grieving has fortunately become an acceptable subject for discussion in the last decade, but even in the 'sixties it was almost taboo. It still seems to be when the grieving is caused by the death of a pet.

Some degree of mourning after a bereavement is, of course, necessary and normal. Pet owners may even be more prone to grieving than non-pet owners. They do, after all, exhibit greater affiliative tendencies on personality tests than non-pet owners, so we would expect them to grieve profoundly when a pet has died. Remember, most people think of their pets as members of the family, and specifically as children under three years of age. The grief of a parent for a child can be the deepest grief of all. But the death of a pet is complicated by an additional factor which plays no part in the death of a relative or friend – in many instances death is a consequence of an active decision by the owners.

I wish that all the dogs and cats and birds and snakes and turtles and rodents and rabbits and fish that I treat would die in their sleep. They don't. The life expectancies of all domestic pets are dramatically increasing, and unless they die traumatically in traffic or other accidents, they are likely to live on to a ripe old age. When they get to a ripe old age, they don't suddenly die. Instead, bits of them age faster than other bits. They go blind or lose the use of their hind legs, or become incontinent, or a myriad of other things. And I have to help the owners make a life and death decision; a decision that is unique to veterinary medicine and a decision which invariably carries with it the seeds of the feeling of guilt.

I kill three out of every two hundred animals that are brought in to me. A survey in the western United States showed that veterinarians there kill four out of every two hundred animals brought to them. None of us say "kill", but that is what is is. The owners of the pets, and many veterinarians, will use euphemisms such as "put to sleep", although these are fraught with the danger of being misinterpreted as meaning simply anaesthetizing.

Legally, pets are, in most Western countries, the property of the owners. As chattels, the owners can do with them as they please, and that includes asking that they be destroyed. In California, a new law that prohibits the malicious or unnecessary destruction of animals was successfully used in June 1980, when a group called Attorneys for Animals' Rights successfully used the law to prevent the destruction of a pet whose owner had stipulated in her Will that the animal be destroyed after her death. I don't know if such a law exists elsewhere. It should. In the meantime, owners can ask veterinarians to kill their pets for the most capricious of reasons.

They can also ask for deadly serious ones. John Sampson, a colleague of mine who practises in Romsey, Hampshire, has recounted to me such an incident.

An elderly and long-standing client of the practice appeared at John's hospital one afternoon and asked that his two pet dogs be destroyed. John was taken aback by the request and asked why. The owner replied that it had been his wife's wish that the dogs be destroyed after she died, and he was simply fulfilling her last wish. John was even more surprised. Romsey is a small town and he was embarrassed that he did not know that the owner's wife had died. He apologized for not knowing and asked when she had passed away. The husband replied that she had died a few hours previously.

Realizsing that now was not the time for this man to make such a decision, John offered to board the animals so that the owner would be free to make the arrangements necessary and cope with everything without worrying about the dogs. The owner politely declined and firmly told John that, although John had always been the dogs' vet and that the dogs were relaxed with him, he would take them elsewhere to be euthanized, even if it meant more distress to the animals. John relented and carried out the owner's wishes. Several hours later the police arrived to ask if John had seen this man that day. He had gone home and committed suicide.

The person who earnestly intends to commit suicide tidies up loose ends before ending his or her existence. The dogs were two loose ends.

The decision to euthanize will vary from veterinarian to veterinarian and from case to case. The decision is not completely dependent upon the well-being of the animal. I remember as a student working during the summer in a veterinary practice in San Francisco, and seeing an old Beagle with heart disease and bone cancer. Bone cancer is painful and, practically-speaking, in old dogs untreatable. But the veterinarian I was assisting, was keeping it on pain killers and other drugs. I asked him why. I didn't think it was fair to the dog. "Look at that man," he said. "He's blind. His son was brought home dead from Vietnam six months ago and his wife died just after that. That old dog is all he has and I'm going to keep it for him just as long as I can."

If the owners had been a young married couple with children, I would have euthanized it because they would have had each other for support and would have eventually replaced the dog. Similarly, if the owners had been "empty nesters", I might have prolonged the decision for a month or so until they were psychologically prepared and then done the deed. But this man was blind. This was his last dog.

Euthanasia is the part of practice I find most difficult. On the surface, it seems the antithesis of what I should be doing. I should be curing, not killing. It has taken a long time to accept that it is a necessary and beneficial act in many instances. I suppose if you do it frequently enough, it should become routine. In the abbattoir business this is actually a management worry, and in the one abbattoir in Kitchener, Ontario, that I had to visit frequently when I worked at the veterinary college's Virus Research Institute, the stick man, the man who actually cut each pig's throat after it had been stunned, was only kept on that job for a limited time before being moved to another part of the plant. I guess the management thought that the routine might just become too routine and if he had a fight with his wife, well. . . .

My wife can still tell by looking at me whether I have had to kill one of my patients. The way it affects me varies with how well I have known the animal and its owners. To some degree, although surprisingly less than I would have thought when I first entered practice, it depends on how much I like the animal and the owners. But it also depends on the specifics of each situation.

Several years ago, a colleague in London found that he had to be away from his practice and asked if I could help him out. All his clients were new to me, but one of them gave me one of the most difficult tasks I ever had to do.

A middle-aged woman brought her nine-year-old West Highland Terrier in because it had been limping for a considerable time and was now crying whenever it moved, and it had not eaten for two days. I feared the worst when I saw the dog. Her left shoulder was swollen and painful to touch. Her colour was poor and she was having difficulty breathing. I took X-rays of the leg and of the chest. The owner – I can't remember her name – preferred not to wait for the results and asked me to telephone her at home later that day.

The results were as I suspected. The Westie had a tumour of its shoulder bone which had spread into the lungs. It must have been there for some time, but all terriers are tough. This dog probably coped well with its disability until the pain and breathing difficulties became unbearable. There was nothing I could do, and even postponing euthanasia would have been unfair.

I telephoned the owner in the early afternoon and explained the gravity of the situation. Sensibly, she knew that the only humane course open was to euthanise her pet. I think she had understood the gravity of the situation before she brought the dog in. She promised to return in the afternoon. I remember that it was a late December day and that it was cold and raining, as London often is at that time of year. Dusk came, and an hour later the owner and the dog arrived. The woman was sodden with rain. She was soaked to the skin, but she wasn't shivering. The dog was dry. I gave her a towel to dry her face and asked her how she got so wet. Every day in the dog's life, she told me, regardless of the weather, she and her dog had walked all the way around Kensington Gardens. The dog couldn't walk now because of its pain, but it was its last day and she said she knew the dog would want to see its territory once more. So she put a blanket in the basket of her bicycle, gently placed the dog on it and took her for one last look. She held an umbrella over the dog so that it would not get wet. She looked at me and the dog looked at me, and tears just rolled down my face. How could I do it? How could I play God?

Most pet owners seem more distressed at the thought of euthanasia than at the thought of death itself. They see it as unnatural. But this could then apply to the other side of the coin as well, in that living with the aid of kidney dialysis or an iron lung could be described as an unnatural life.

People very often write to me after their pet has died, or has had its life ended. It is a response to a letter of condolence that I send on those occasions. These letters very often tell me things that I wish I had known when the pet was still alive. In relation to euthanasia the response can be summed up by a letter I once received: "I bawled my eyes out more than I thought possible, but I'm glad she died naturally and didn't have to be put down. That would have seemed much worse."

The decision to end a pet's life is one that is best made jointly by the owners and their veterinarian. Bernard Hershhorn, a veterinarian in New York City, gives six criteria to help owners make a decision. He asks them to ask themselves the following questions:

1. Is the condition prolonged, recurring or getting worse?
2. Is the condition no longer responsive to therapy?
3. Is the animal in pain or otherwise suffering physically?

4. Is it no longer possible to alleviate that pain or suffering?
5. If your pet should recover, is it likely to be chronically ill, an invalid, or unable to care for itself as a healthy animal can?
6. If your pet recovers, is it likely no longer to be able to enjoy life, or will it have severe personality changes?

Hershhorn says that if the answer to all of these questions is "yes" then euthanasia should be undertaken. If the answer to three or four of them is "no", then the pet should be permitted to die naturally, but the following questions should first be answered by the owner:

1. Can you provide the necessary care?
2. Will such care interfere with your own life so as to create serious problems for you or your family?
3. Will the cost involved become unbearably expensive?

Hershhorn's criteria are a sound basis for making a decision concerning euthanasia, but there is one more important factor which must be considered. "Are there any family members who are emotionally dependent on the animal?" If there are, I want to know about it. A decision such as this should be a family decision. Children should have the situation explained to them. Parents who try to protect the children by telling them that they are just taking the pet to the vet can be doing more harm than good. I have seen problems arise because the child has felt that the parents simply wanted to get rid of the dog.

I would suggest that the following are among the valid reasons for ending a pet's life:

1. Overwhelming physical injury.
2. Irreversible disease that has progressed to a point where distress or discomfort cannot be controlled.
3. Old-age wear and tear that permanently affects the "quality of life".
4. Physical injury, disease or wear and tear resulting in permanent loss of control of body functions.
5. Aggressiveness with risk to children, owners or others.

6. The carrying of untreatable disease dangerous to humans.

I am asked to kill pets for many reasons, but as far as I am concerned, few of them are valid.

Most people I meet through practice do not understand what is done; how a life is ended. Veterinarians invariably euthanize pets by using a concentrated form of anaesthetic. The barbiturate is given in a vein; a procedure many pets have experienced before with other injectables. Unconsciousness occurs almost instantaneously and death within seconds. I ask the owners if they want to stay while this is done, and most do to tickle their pets' heads or to talk to them. They see that it is a peaceful procedure; a good death. Many who don't stay want to return to see the body. I guess it adds reality to the situation. It might even be beneficial for children to do so. Children who have not had any experience of death may be helped by seeing that the animal is not breathing, to understand what death is.

Grieving after the death of a pet is poorly understood, but strongly felt. Richard Joseph wrote *A Letter to the Man Who Killed My Dog* in 1957. Let me quote a short section from it.

> *"The vet looked at me, then I put my arm around my wife and led her out to the car. We talked on the way home but our voices sounded strange to each other, and we didn't really say anything. I think we must have felt as parents do when they have lost a child. . . . I am not a man who cries easily, but picking up her bone and her rubber ball, her food and water dishes, I cried as I haven't cried since childhood. I'm glad my wife wasn't there to see me cry that way, because I would have had to stop then, and the hurt within me would have been worse."*

The way Richard Joseph felt was the same as the way Mary Stewart felt when her daughter died. Mary, an American veterinarian who teaches at the University of Glasgow, has written the only published paper comparing grieving at the loss of a pet and of a child.

Mary's daughter, a veterinary student who suffered from

anorexia nervosa, committed suicide when she was twenty-one years old. As a means of catharsis, Mary wrote down, after Edie's death, how she felt immediately after the event, and afterwards. Later on, using this as a basis, she did two things. First, point by point, she compared her feelings at her daughter's death with her feelings when she lost a pet. Second, she arranged through a school teacher friend that sixty-five younger children, seventy older children and forty adults write down in their own words how they had felt or thought they would feel when their pets died.

Half of the younger children mentioned they were "upset" or "very upset" when their pets died, although half of these said they were "not so sad now". And over half of all the youngsters mentioned that other animals were helpful in getting them over their sadness.

This was not the case with the older children. Sixty-five per cent were either upset or very upset when their pets died, but only 7% said that they were helped by having other animals. The older children also felt anger or resentment.

Some were angry that their parents had had the pet destroyed. Some felt guilty that they had not looked after the pet properly when it was alive. They said things like "I knew him all my life", and "His death ended my childhood".

Farley Mowat finished his recollection of childhood with his dog Mutt this way. "There was no other wanderer on that road, yet I was not alone, for his tracks went with me, each pawprint as familiar as the print of my own hand. I followed them, and I knew each thing that he had done, each move that he had made, each thought that had been his; for so it is with two who live one life together.

"I returned directly to the road, and my boots were sucking in the mud when a truck came howling along towards me and passed in a shower of muddy water. I glanced angrily after it, for the driver had almost hit me in his blind rush. As I watched, it swerved sharply to make a bend in the road and vanished from my view. I heard the sudden shrilling of brakes, then the roar of an accelerating motor – and it was gone.

"I did not know that, in its passing, it had made an end to the best years that I had lived."

Aaron Katcher says that in late childhood or young adulthood "the death of a pet becomes a kind of rite of passage, a symbol of the loss of animal innocence, animal itself."

The adults' responses were more complicated still. Over half said they had guilt feelings over the death of the pet. All were sad, but some were so distressed that they said they found it difficult to speak or to cope with work, or even to eat. In describing how she felt when her daughter died, Mary said that to speak felt as though she had to squeeze the words past an obstruction in her throat.

Over half the adults were comforted by other animals, either pets that were there, or ones introduced after the death. But all the individuals who experienced prolonged grieving were reluctant to get another pet for a considerable time.

Those pet owners who held a simple ceremony for their pet felt comforted by it. Mary says that the ritual involved after Edie died was comforting to her. It gave her a sense of support and "oneness" with others. The Royal Society for

the Prevention of Cruelty to Animals produces a booklet called *Service of Prayer for Animals*, and I know of pets I have looked after who have been buried with full religious ceremony. This is shaky ground for some. The Catholic Church, for example, says that only the human has a soul. There are feats of mental dexterity that one can employ to get around this, however. When a client, a vicar, lost his pet Boston Terrier recently, he wrote to me, "Many years ago when an adored dog died, a great friend, a Bishop, said to me, 'You must always remember that, as far as the Bible is concerned, God only threw the humans out of Paradise.'"

Ritual reinforces the cyclical nature of life. Repetition of the same procedures for the same reasons helps to imprint on us the continuum of life and death. The 18 November 1981, edition of *The Times* carried the story of such a ritual. Charlie, the ship's cat at HMS *Pembroke* offices at Chatham Naval Base in Kent, was buried with full naval honours. The bugler played the Last Post, the flag was lowered to half mast and the officer of the watch read the service. When the Chief Petty Officer was asked why this had been done, he replied simply that the cat had been "a full member of the crew".

The end of a life is the end only for that person. Friends and relatives experience a protracted and painful process in which that life is only given up gradually and after a struggle. Mary says, "My mind kept trying to jump back in time to the point before I knew (that Edie died), as if my ignorance of the fact would make it disappear, as if my acceptance would give it substance." Pet owners react in exactly the same way when their pets die suddenly. "Don't say it," I am told when I return to them after a failed attempt at trying to restart a heart. "I don't want to hear it." The initial denial of the death is similar.

Memories of the lost pet may be sharpened for a short while. Konrad Lorenz, the ethologist, described it this way, in 1957 in his book *Man Meets Dog*: "In the weeks immediately following Bully's death I really began to understand what it is that makes naïve people believe in the ghosts of the dead. The constant sound throughout seventeen years of the dog trotting at my heels had left such a lasting impression on my brain that for weeks afterwards, as if with my own ears, I heard him pattering after me."

Mary Stewart's findings are consistent with a survey carried out by the American magazine *Cat Fancy* on *Handling the Death of a Pet*. The magazine had over two thousand replies to their survey. Over 75% reported feeling deeply distraught over the deaths of their own pets. The one-third of the respondents who had to make a decision to euthanize their pets felt more guilt than did the others. Most of these people said that one of the hardest parts of the experience was finding someone who could understand their feelings and to whom they could talk. Most respondents reported that friends and relatives just didn't understand their grief.

One reader, almost paraphrasing Richard Joseph, wrote: "My husband and I left the vet's office and cried all the way home. Tom's reaction was surprising to him. 'If someone had told me several years ago,' he said, 'that I would cry over the death of a cat I would have called him a liar'." Another wrote: "We buried her in a special box with one of my husband, Frank's, old T-shirts that she loved, and tucked a piece of lace from my wedding dress in her paw (she died exactly one month after our wedding day). Just as I was covering her and closing the box, Frank appeared with one of her favourite toys. I have never been so touched by a simple gesture. I hadn't been crying but I started then. We cried together. Even in death, Jennie brought us a little closer."

Gradually, however, ever so gradually, the animal is, bit by bit and memory by memory, given up. It is only when this occurs that healing can take place and a new pet can replace the old. The length of time that this process takes will vary from person to person and family to family. Because pets are often euthanized, the process of grieving can begin even before the animal dies. Owners often know, either because their veterinarian has told them or because they are astute enough to see that their pet has only a limited time to live. Grieving can start then, and can be softened by the presence of another pet.

There are similarities between grieving at the loss of a pet and grieving at the loss of a person, but there are also great differences. The loss of a child permanently changes your life. Mary Stewart calls it an "earth stopper". The loss of a pet temporarily changes the quality of your life. Whereas there is sadness over the potential that will never be realized when a child dies, the sadness when a pet dies is due more to the personal loss.

There are differences, too, that make grieving over the death of a pet more difficult. With human deaths, all the practical aspects and decisions are taken care of by the medical staff, but with an animal the owners must first decide if its life is to be ended, and if so, who is to do it, when should it be done, where should it be done and who should be present.

In compassionate surroundings, human death brings to those who are grieving an open and genuine support from others. It's a time of maximum communication. It's a busier time than normal. Friends and relatives are more open and less inhibited than they otherwise are. And, of course, there is ritual and ceremony. All of these things help those who are grieving. They give both physical and mental support.

But such is not the case when a pet dies. In fact, it is sometimes the reverse. People are embarrassed to commiserate with someone whose pet has died. If anything, there is probably less communication then normal. The routine of the rest of the family is expected to continue, with simply a void where the pet used to be. The barriers that come down when a human dies, if anything, go up when a pet dies. Instead of visitors, telegrams, 'phone calls, letters and flowers, there is loneliness.

A medical practitioner, writing in the British Medical Journal, recounted such an instance this way.

A lady visited his surgery because she was unhappy. The practitioner, a man named Elliot-Binns, asked her to make a list of what was troubling her. She wrote down that her husband was made redundant, that her baby cried a lot, her neighbour was rude, and her dog had died. As she wrote that down, tears flowed.

People simply don't like to admit that they are grieving. They look upon it as a sign of weakness. My children haven't had the problem. They have been able to bury their dead goldfish with full and elaborate funerals.

Elliot-Binns went on to describe how his own dog died. It was euthanized by his veterinarian, while it lay under an apple tree in its own garden, eating a chocolate bar. It was buried by a wall in the same garden, with a plaque on the wall above the grave that said, "Beware – ferocious dog"; a plaque that the family had previously bought to boost the dog's morale. It was all a simple little exercise in bereavement, and softened the sadness of losing an important member of the family.

One aspect of coping with the death of a pet is easier. My dog is very special to me because through her I met my wife. She has symbolic value as well as "dog" value. Her symbolic value isn't replaceable, but her "dog" value, to a great extent, is. Although I, like most other owners, like to think my pet is unique, as a veterinarian I know that the traits I like in my dog can be found elsewhere. She has the standard traits of a female Golden Retriever; softness of mouth and of temperament, gentleness and a willingness and desire to exercise and play retrieving games. It is an easily trainable and clean breed, and with luck, after she dies, if I want to replace her "dog" value, I need only carefully select another female Golden Retriever pup who shows aspects of the same temperament.

The pet owner is burdened with one other problem which is unique to a person who has lost a pet. That is a feeling of embarrassment. Well-meaning friends often try to help owners over the loss of their pet by saying "Don't worry about it too much. It was only a dog (or cat). You can get another one soon." Trivialization of the death can heighten the feeling of embarrassment that one feels. Sometimes this embarrassment can get out of hand and actually create medical problems.

Michael McCulloch, a psychiatrist in Portland, Oregon, has told me of such a case that he has encountered. Michael had referred to him for counselling a young man, a middle-class high school student. This person had been an academic high achiever, but his academic performance started to deteriorate about a month after his pet German Shepherd died accidentally, and after another month his academic performance was so poor that it was a cause for concern in his family and at his school. Although it appeared at first that he was grieving over the loss of the pet, it transpired that both his personality and performance changes were related to his feeling of shame and embarrassment that he could feel such grief for what was "only a dog".

The people I see who are at risk of developing a pathological degree of grief and mourning when their pets die are those who are emotionally dependent on their pets, or those who insist on a special relationship with them. I can see it coming with animals that still are young and healthy, let alone those that are old and infirm. I see one Yorkshire Terrier who should, by rights, be dead already but, because of the perseverance of the owner, is alive and active, relatively toothless, but "all there".

This little dog was born with an incomplete brain. The part of the brain called the cerebellum was not developed completely, and the pup as a consequence could not orient itself. If left alone, it would simply roll until it hit something. I suggested that it be destroyed, for it had a severe defect, but the owners asked if anything could be done. I knew that, in kittens suffering from this problem, if they lived to ten weeks of age other parts of the brain could take over the functions of the absent parts and the animal would be able to stand and learn to walk. I told them this, and they decided that they wanted to do everything they could to save him. This meant hand rearing the pup, and for the next month the owners fed it, initially every two hours, stimulated it to urinate and defecate by massaging the genital region with warm, wet cotton wool, and helped it to learn proper orientation by developing a special sling so that it could be "walked". The dog did get better and, except for infrequent epileptic attacks, it is now quite normal. The owner's marriage wasn't as successful. In the absence of children, this little dog has taken on paramount importance to the woman. She hasn't had a holiday in six years because she is fearful that something might happen to it if she goes away. And she carries it everywhere. I've started preparing her now for its eventual demise, but I know there will be trouble ahead. She has made a great emotional investment in the dog, and will receive unwanted dividends in the end.

Mary Stewart's work has shown that, in circumstances of emotional dependency on a pet, bereavement can take on all the aspects of human bereavement. It can be the real "earth-stopper", with an inability to speak, loss of appetite, an inability to cope with usual responsibilities, and depression. For these people there is the additional deleterious fact that there is little of the support available which usually surrounds a human bereavement, such as the sharing of grief and acknowledgement of loss. These people are very often emotionally dependent on their pets, in the first place, because of an already existing deficiency in contact, involvement and support from other people. There are many instances where I know that my nurses and I are the only support that is available to these people.

The psychiatrist E. K. Rynearson has reported several cases of pathological grieving. In an article in the *British Journal of Psychiatry*, he reported this one. A forty-year-old woman came to see him suffering from an unusually intense and prolonged grief reaction following the death of her dog. Seven years previously she had developed exophthalmic goitre, and subsequently became terribly self-conscious about the changes to her facial appearance. She became very reclusive, seldom venturing out of the house. Her son's and her husband's support and reassurance were of no value. Instead, she turned to her dog for support. She said, "for some reason he was the only thing that seemed to matter to me." Her need for the dog increased and it slept with her at night. "We were never out of each other's sight until he died," she said. But after the dog died she was forced to seek help. Rynearson says that the origins of her compulsive care-giving to the dog were in her childhood. Her earliest memories were of caring for her ailing mother, whose morbid fear of illness created an atmosphere of imminent separation. That complicated relationship continued to exist, and when she developed her goitre she said of her mother, "when my eyes started to change – it would hurt her too much to look at me." The mother, in fact, did find the changes unbearable. This lady's intense attachment to her pet was a reaction to the stresses of her own illness, combined with her mother's fearful reaction to illness in general. It stirred in her a preconditioned ambivalence towards human attachments. She was more trusting of the unconditional caring and care-giving with her pet than with the people surrounding her. And because of this excessive reliance on her pet, a reliance which existed in conjunction with the fact that she had no meaningful human relationships, she suffered from excessive mourning. Kenneth Keddie, a Scottish psychiatrist, says, "The greater the degree to which the pet animal has been forced into a 'quasi-human' role during its lifetime, the greater will be the risk that the owner will suffer a devastating and possibly emotionally damaging type of reaction after the pet has been put to sleep or accidentally killed." E. K. Rynearson says the same thing, but with bigger words. "Under abnormal circumstances of developmental frustration," he says, "humans may displace the over-determined need for attachment to a pet. This attachment relationship is pathological because of its defensive purpose and its interruption can create an enduring psychiatric reaction."

Anyone can suffer from this, but because the elderly frequently live alone, they are more at risk of using their pets as surrogate people. One elderly lady wrote to me, only to ask for advice about ridding her cat of fleas, but her letter contained an explicit statement of her anxious attachment to her cat. "He is dear to me," she wrote, "more than I can ever express – my dearest companion – the only one, and the dread (of losing him), which is very real, is an ever present nightmare." To nurture or be nurtured is a normal need. But when there are no other humans available to do either, our pets can act as surrogates. Some people have an increased need to nurture and be nurtured all their lives, and these are the people who are at risk of developing dependent relationships with their pets. If they do develop dependent relationships they can become over-anxious about anything, even the risk of losing the pet because it has a flea infestation. Compulsive care-giving is another manifestation of the fear of separation. John Bowlby, the psychologist who developed, and has written the most extensively on, "attachment theory", says of the compulsive care-giver that his or her craving for attachment is satisfied by acting as a source of nurture rather than as the recipient. "The person who develops in this way has found that the only affectional bond available is one in which he must always be the care giver, and that the only care he can ever receive is the care he gives."

Both the pet owner who is anxiously attached to the pet and the pet owner who compulsively cares for the pet suffer from, to some extent, a developmentally induced distrust of human attachments. If other human attachments are available but not utilized, then these people could be said to have a basic distrust of human attachments. They displace their attachment to their pets, who are, of course, consistently receptive to it. To quote Ogden Nash:

I marvel that such
Small ribs as these
Can cage such vast
Desire to please.

It is an intense emotional investment, and the loss, or even anticipated loss, of the pet can create complicated and sometimes prolonged psychiatric reactions.

Kenneth Keddie feels that pathological grieving is most common in relation to small pets. As small animals are

frequently chosen to be the objects of excessive care-giving
he may be correct, although I have seen excessive grieving in
owners of animals of all sizes. Bereavement is a painful
process. Sometimes it is suppressed and not worked out.
Occasionally I see a client who grieves excessively and in a
prolonged fashion after his or her pet has died, but who I
know has "coped so well" when his or her spouse has died
recently. It bothered me at one time that some people could
cope so well with the death of a husband, for example, but
then fall to pieces when the pet poodle died a year later. What
I didn't know at that time was that these people were "double
mourning".

"Double mourning" occurs when the normal grieving
process is, for whatever the reasons may be, suppressed on
one occasion but then manifested on another. Mrs Cohen's
husband died early last year from cancer of the liver. I had
known for some time that he was dying and thought that
Mrs Cohen was magnificent in the way she threw herself into
charity activities after he died. But nine months later her
yellow Labrador was losing weight, retching occasionally and
becoming increasingly lethargic. The laboratory investi-
gations showed that its liver which was palpably enlarged
was failing. The inevitable conclusion was that her dog was
dying, and possibly from cancer of the liver as well. Mrs
Cohen was incredulous. She simply would not believe that
her dog was dying, and specifically of liver disease. She
would not accept the similar advice of a second opinion, and
a third was arranged. During this time she ceased her charity
work so that she could be with her dog. It died naturally; I
had no need to intervene, and she chose to bury it herself. A
Labrador is a big dog, and I worried about her physical
ability to dig its grave, but she would not allow anyone else
to do it, or even to help. For months afterwards friends of
hers would tell me that she talked of nothing but her dog. Its
life was central to her thoughts, and apparently paramount to
her husband's memory. Her real problem was that she had
simply not permitted herself to grieve normally when her
husband died. And there is no way that you can avoid that
emotional burden. If it is suppressed it will surface elsewhere
at some time. Mrs Cohen was really experiencing the grief

that she had suppressed when her husband died, as well as the grief at losing a pet who was a remaining living contact with her husband. The older, unresolved loss was being worked through at the same time.

Many doctors understand how people can grieve when a pet dies. Unfortunately, not all are so sympathetic. One such doctor wrote this little anecdote recently in *Pulse*, a newspaper for doctors in Britain: "During surgery one evening in July we had a thunderstorm that caused a lot of flooding. When I finished I had to visit a child with persistent asthma. I found I had to paddle through 12 inch deep water to get to the house.

The last time it flooded like that in our town, many of the roads were still unmade – it was 12 years ago – and my partner was on holiday. I was busy, so I wasn't too happy when the call came to see an old lady, who had been taken ill, at the end of one of these unmade roads. I plodded off down the path. The water lapped over my wellingtons. I was soaked when I got to her house. And she looked quite well. I asked her what the problem was. She said, 'My budgie's died and I feel very upset about it.'

I have never forgiven her for that episode, but she's still on my list."

The problems of grieving or excessive grieving do not apply only to pet owners. People ask me if their pets will suffer when their dog or cat or human companions die. Of course they do, and sometimes even their grief can be pathological. This story was recently recounted to me before I first saw the Alsatian referred to in the letter. Heidi's problems developed after its Jack Russell companion died:

"When Heidi joined our household she was 'taken over' by my Jack Russell, a crafty, courageous, clever little dog, getting on a little but determined to run the world his way. She adored him, had confidence in him, and would go anywhere so long as he was there. He recognized in her good exploitation material for doing things he was getting too old for, like chasing the tradesmen, and tried to inaugurate her into his wicked ways. As his arthritis got worse, he would jump into her basket to keep himself warm, pushing her well over to the side and

growling if she moved – and she would lie still for hours just to keep him warm. His last party trick before he died used to be to creep under the dining room table before a smart dinner party, to wait until everyone was seated and enjoying themselves, and to smartly nip the first foot to move. A howl of agony would then interrupt the conversation and Trigger would be hustled from the room, shaking his sides with laughter, his wicked beady little eyes gleaming. Heidi would be anxiously waiting in the hall to nuzzle him, while he explained triumphantly that he'd done it again. This was the relationship. He made her laugh. He made her feel important and they were always together. (After he died) she missed him so terribly, although she is never parted from me. She has suffered terrible bowel trouble and latterly has begun urinating in her sleep. She and I have a very deep love for one another, but I am sad that even I have not been able to restore her confidence."

This dog's urinary incontinence and bowel problems were resolved when they were treated with anti-anxiety drugs. Although it can equally be argued that the dog was anxious because of the owner's reaction to Trigger's death, it is more likely that it was grieving over the loss of its "leader".

Last month another client wrote to me describing his cat's behaviour after the senior cat in the household died. Although the letter shows that he is still in the denial stage of his own grieving, it gives a fascinating insight into cat behaviour:

"For the first three days (after Ming's death) Chan and Mitsou looked everywhere for him, and expected us every time that we came back into the flat, having been out, to bring him back. After three days the pattern changed. Ming always sat or lay in a particular place on the left of the fireplace. Now neither of the two other cats will sit there, or even walk across it. They laid out Ming's favourite toys there – (two pink catnip mice) – and they sit for hours on the other side of the fireplace apparently 'talking' to something that we cannot see. They have both completely calmed down, but they are upset if anybody moves Ming's mice. To see what would happen, we have deliberately moved these and put them elsewhere in the room at night before going to bed – but the next morning they are back in their

proper place, and they are there now as I write. Nor do the cats like anybody standing there, and on occasions I have done so to light the fire and, looking up, have seen expressions of horror on the cats' faces, as if I was treading on Ming. The same thing has happened to my wife and to the girl who comes in twice a week to help keep the place clean.

"I have the very distinct impression that dear old Ming is still about. One thing is certain, nobody can sit in his place, or move his mice. If any of us stands there this is regarded with horror, and if we move his toys these are brought back and placed in his place.

"I do hope the old boy is still about, as we miss him dreadfully. I only wish that we could see him again. I thought you might be interested."

Perhaps Ming's ghost really is there. But if a ghost is there, what has happened to its soul? Silliness perhaps, but to a religious person who loves his pet, what happens to the pet's soul after death can create a moral dilemma. The Catholic church denies that animals have souls, yet it has regularly excommunicated them. In the Middle Ages even a swarm of crop-destroying locusts was excommunicated in France. Animals were prosecuted in British and European courts until the 19th century. We have a problem in developing a moral attitude towards pets and in categorizing their rights.

Many years ago, an estate agent burst into my clinic in great distress, carrying a travel kennel containing a twelve week old West Highland Terrier. The estate agent had found the pup while showing a prospective purchaser a flat in Central London. The cage was soiled with blood, faeces and urine. There was dried blood on the corners where the pup had tried to chew its way out. The pup's lips were torn and there were slivers of wood embedded in its gums. It was dehydrated and emaciated. It flamboyantly wagged its tail and tried to lick my hand, but its head was too heavy to lift and its mouth was too dry. It died shortly after.

The pup had been left in the cage in the flat seventeen days before when the previous tenant had returned to Kuwait. He bought the pup to take home to Kuwait with him, but before leaving decided he did not want it and left it to die.

Does a pet have a right to life? Does a pet have a moral right to die with dignity? A pet's rights are poorly defined. People ask me to kill their pets because they are moving. They ask me to kill their animals because they cannot house-train them. They ask me to kill them because the pets grow up and are not as much fun, or because they become too expensive to care for. A group of lawyers in San Francisco has recognized this void in the law and, calling themselves Attorneys for Animal Rights, they take on legal cases which challenge the traditional legal view that animals are the property of humans, to be bought and sold, used and abused, strictly for human convenience. They say that anti-cruelty laws at present only punish deviant human behaviour rather than protect animals.

Bronson La Follette, the attorney general of Wisconsin, has shown how ill-defined animal rights laws are. La Follette was cited by the police for letting Cutter, his Irish Setter, run loose in Madison, Wisconsin. Through his attorney, La Follette got the charges reduced each time they went to court. The first time he demanded a jury of Cutter's peers, and brought twelve dogs into court. On his second appearance he put Cutter in a line-up with several other Irish Setters and asked the dog catcher to identify Cutter. He could not. On the third occasion, La Follette's lawyer argued that not allowing Cutter to run free on occasion amounted to "cruel and unusual punishment" and was constitutionally unfair. La Follette approached the subject of his dog's legal rights with whimsy and humour. Bernard Rollins examines the animal's moral rights in a similar, but serious fashion.

Bernard Rollins teaches Moral Philosophy in Veterinary Medicine to veterinary students at Colorado State University. He says he is particularly proud of the benefit his lectures have had on cows' rectums. He explains it this way. While a faculty member in the Department of Philosophy at the University, he somehow convinced the veterinary administration to permit him to give a series of lectures on ethics to veterinary students. Now, I remember as a veterinary student that if underwater basket weaving had been on the curriculum I might have complained a little, but if it meant taking it to pass, then so be it.

Rollins felt that attitude from his students when he started his lectures, but by the eighth week students were actually asking for more. Can you imagine? With all they had to learn in medicine and surgery, pharmacology, epidemiology, physiology and clinical pathology, they wanted even more! Rollins had touched a raw nerve, latent in almost all veterinary students. Day in and day out. Cause and effect. Etiology and pathology. Diagnosis and treatment. But what about the patient? What about pain? What about suffering? At university we were preoccupied with fact. Perhaps more than in any other science, veterinary medicine is the study of fact. Unending conveyor belt fact. The gestation period of a pig is three months, three weeks and three days. The rumen of a cow can hold 40 gallons. Cerebellar hypoplasia in cats can be caused by panleukopenia virus and may be transmitted transplacentally. Progressive retinal atrophy can appear in the Schnauzer as early as six months, but in the Golden Retriever may not appear until five years. Von Gierke's syndrome has only been diagnosed in the Yorkshire Terrier. But what about the patient! That is what was eating at Rollins' students. And Rollins' lectures brought that out. What is proper and improper? What research using animals can be condoned and what research should be criticized? Should a veterinary school sponsor a rodeo? Who should act as a conscience for animals? How often should a clinical training procedure be performed on the same animal?

Before long, Rollins found himself in the position, in a sense, of faculty ombudsman for animals. He was asked to attend the school rodeo and assess the events in terms of cruelty. He became involved, at the students' instigation, in the well-being of research animals and, among other things, worked to increase the number of cows used to teach rectal palpation, for determining pregnancy, to veterinary students. Rollins broke into a broad, toothy grin when he told me that, as a graduate student in philosophy at Columbia University, he never dreamt that he would put his training to work for the benefit of cows' rectums. More importantly, until Rollins, there was no emphasis on moral and social concerns in veterinary training. As in medicine, it was thought that the moral and social implications of what we do would be picked up in practice. Unfortunately, this doesn't usually happen. What does happen is that the problem is ignored.

Eskimos used to lay the head of a deceased dog in a child's grave so that the soul of the dog, which is everywhere at home, would guide the helpless infant to the land of the souls.

Some cultures do have an animal morality developed into their traditions. We don't. And because we don't have cultural guidelines on how to react when a pet dies, or what innate rights a pet has, we have a problem in deciding what our personal response should be. We should regard the keeping of pets as a privilege, not as a right. We should accept that with that privilege we take on responsibilities for their care. But we should be careful in not using pets as a conduit for channelling our feelings and emotions the wrong way. The pet is not a panacea for all human ills, and indeed those who lean heavily on their pets for emotional support harm their pets as much as themselves. Pragmatically, there are those who will continue to need to do so. Boris Levinson, a psychiatrist, acknowledged this in his book *Pets and Human Development* when he wrote: "It would undoubtedly be preferable for all children to be brought up in homes by attentive, loving, understanding parents or parent surrogates and for old people to live out their days in their own familiar surroundings, cared for physically and emotionally, and given an honoured place in society. It would be better if society were not so mechanized, routinized and cut of from the vital rhythms of the natural world. But this is not the reality of life, at least in the western world, and far-reaching improvements will be a long time in coming. In the meantime, animals can provide some relief, give much pleasure, and remind us of our origins."

In their dying as much as in their living, pets can enrich our lives and teach us much about our own nature. The succession of animals in a pet owner's life seems tragic, but it need not be. All of us must eventually meet with, and accept the inevitability of, the death of loved ones, and of our own demise. The repetition of birth, life and death in our pets during our lives can help us to understand better the constancy of our existence, the constancy of the cycles of life. Just as the seasons change and a spring will never be the same, there will always be another one. So it is with life. We can learn and accept the constancy of nature through a succession of animals. They can also give us a symbolic image of natural perfection. Lord Byron wrote this epitaph when a friend of his died:

"Near this spot are deposited the remains of one who possessed beauty without vanity, strength without insolence, courage without ferocity, and all the virtues of man without his vices. This praise, which would be unmeaning flattery if inscribed over human ashes, is but a just tribute to the memory of Boatswain, a dog."

CHAPTER SIX

Pet related problems

Sixty-six tons of dog faeces are dropped on the streets, parks, gardens and pavements of London daily. If you are a Londoner that is a problem. A Newfoundlander, however, may not consider sixty-six tons of dog faeces in London to be a severe problem. Newfoundlanders complain about cow droppings on their sidewalks because in that province there exists a "free range" law with its concomitant aesthetic result. They also complain about bears chasing them when they go berry picking, and of moose on the Queen's Highway. In fact, moose create other problems as well. The Newfoundland Humane Society receives complaints that moose are eating cabbages. The moose, with its long legs, can easily step over most fences and apparently has the habit of taking one bite out of each cabbage; in doing so it can destroy one acre of a market gardener's patch in a night.

My reason for mentioning the problems Newfoundlanders complain of is to explain that the problems that animals create will vary from place to place. Dog faeces, dogs barking and dogs chasing cars are a worry to the Newfoundlander, too, but in Britain, certainly at the moment, dog faeces is the subject that seems to being out the most vitriolic debate. Although it is an aesthetic problem, it is in part camouflaged by a lot of sensationalism attached to the disease implications that it carries. When I was a young teenager, masturbation was supposed to be the greatest cause of blindness. Now it's dog dung!

Thirty years ago it was discovered that the common dog roundworm, *Toxocara canis*, was a health hazard to people.

For a human to be infected, however, we need three factors. First, there must be a young dog who is passing *Toxocara* eggs in its faeces. Second, there must be a suitable environment for the incubation of the eggs. There is no *Toxocara canis* infection in dogs in northern Canada, for example, probably because of the climate, but Hyde Park in London, on the other hand, is heaven for the eggs. Third, there must be a person who is liable to swallow dirt from the contaminated environment. Testing soil samples in both the United States and in Britain has shown that between 10% and 20% of soil samples from public parks are contaminated.

The problems that animals create will vary from place to place

Probably between 2% and 4% of the population has actually swallowed *Toxocara* eggs, but this does not mean that they have suffered any medical consequence as a result. Anyone with a properly working immune defence system will isolate the larvae and they will cause no harm. A number of children have had eyes removed because of *Toxocara* larvae encysting in them, but this was done essentially because of misdiagnosis. The visible mass in the retina was mistaken for a potentially dangerous tumour called a retinal blastoma. The granuloma that a roundworm larva stimulates looks like the dangerous blastoma but will gradually disappear if it is left alone.

There is a risk, however, to people whose immune systems do not work propertly. A recent survey in Montreal showed that 4% of the population had antibody reactions to roundworms, and by inference, had ingested them. But 22% of asthmatic children had positive reactions and 16% of epileptic children were positive when they were tested. What this means is that *Toxocara* larvae may somehow stimulate an allergic sensitivity to other things.

Visceral larva migrans, the human counterpart of canine roundworm is, nevertheless, an exceptionally rare disease. In the two years after it was made a notifiable disease in New York City, only one case was reported. And it is a problem that can actually be tackled.

Canine waste laws now exist and are enforced in Los Angeles, Minneapolis, Phoenix, Kansas City, Denver, Chicago, Washington and New York. Comparable laws are not as yet enforced in any large cities in Britain. New York's canine waste law was probably the one that received most publicity. On the day the Bill was passed to the Senate, the New York Times noted, "The Assembly passed and sent to the Senate a Bill requiring dog owners in New York City to clean up after their pets on penalty of a fine. The bill also applies to Buffalo." Lest you think that New Yorkers have the problems that Newfoundlanders have with cattle, I should mention that the law was a State law and applied to all cities in New York State with a population of more than 400,000. The City of Buffalo is the only other urban area of that size.

Cleaning up after your dog passes its faeces is simple to do and a logical preventative measure. *Toxocara* eggs are not infectious until three to six weeks after they are passed, so removing faeces will prevent the environment from being seeded. Worming pet dogs is equally important, and although at present most worming medicines licensed for use in dogs only kill worms in the intestinal tract, there are other drugs, originally developed for use in livestock, but now licensed for use in dogs, that not only kill the adult worms in the intestine, but also destroy the larvae in the dog's tissue.

Stooping and scooping laws, although passed on the pretence of the public health hazard that dog faeces create, are really there because of the aesthetic insult that dog dung gives to our environment. Visceral larva migrans is an abstract disease. Scraping shit off your shoes is simply offensive and unpleasant. And the owners of dogs that are allowed to urinate and defecate where they please are downright anti-social.

New York and other cities have tried to cure an aesthetic problem through legislation and have been reasonably successful. Cities like London need New York's approach. It's not impossible to change people's habits. My father cleans up after his dog because the environment he now lives in requires it, yet for the seventy-five years of dog ownership that preceded it there was no compunction to do so. My nurses patrol the pavement outside the clinic each day and clean up whatever droppings are there, lest we be accused of sullying the neighbourhood. It is a simple thing to do and removes one small blight from the environment.

There are other diseases that dogs and cats can transmit, rabies being one and hydatid disease another, and there are almost yearly scientific suggestions of new ones. The current zoonotic equivalent of the flavour of the month is a bacteria called *campylobacter*, which causes a painful and often bloody diarrhoea in people, and can also be found in dog and cat faeces, although it is not known whether it causes a similar disease in these animals. The main source of infection in people is through unpasteurized milk, but incidents of severe diarrhoea in people and pets in the same household should be reported to the family physician and the family veterinarian.

Several years ago, I participated in a televison programme concerning *Toxocara* disease in children, and on that programme the mother of an epileptic child forcefully explained how contact with dog faeces had resulted in her daughter's epilepsy. I spoke to the mother afterwards, and later to the treating physician at the Great Ormonde Street Hospital. There was something not quite right with the episode. This was confirmed when the physician explained that the child suffered from epilepsy as a result of toxoplasmosis, not *Toxocara*. The television programme invited me back to correct the error that had been made. As the cat plays a significant role in the spread of toxoplasmosis, perhaps a brief explanation of it is in order.

The condition of toxoplasmosis has been known about in the human and in other animals for over seventy years.

Perhaps 30% of the population host the condition. I am using the word "condition" intentionally, because in most cases there is no recognizable disease or illness.

Infection with Toxoplasma occurs by eating food contaminated with living organisms. If the person happens to be a pregnant women, the parasite can enter the foetus and cause brain damage to the unborn child. So where do cats fit in? Well, it's a little complicated, but this is what happens.

When a cat is first infected, it passes the organisms in its faeces. If this cat is a barn cat, these organisms may be deposited in cattle feed and once the cattle have eaten this feed, the organisms are stored as dormant and microscopic cysts in the animal's muscle. If people then consume this meat in a lightly cooked state, the disease is passed on to them. This is the most common way in which we are infected.

If a woman is pregnant, there are two things she should do then. She should avoid undercooked meat during her pregnancy. This is the most common source of infection. And she should also arrange with her veterinarian that her cat be checked for toxoplasmosis. Any properly equipped public health laboratory in the UK will do this test. Although I have yet to have a positive result back from the laboratory, it is a simple preventive measure that the veterinarian can take.

. . . allergic to all livestock except chickens

A much more difficult problem that pets can create is that of allergy to them. Let me profess a greater than theoretical interest. As a child I suffered from hay fever and when I was ten years old I was sent to hospital for skin tests because of an acute episode of asthma. My parents received a report indicating that I was allergic to all livestock except chickens, all domestic pets, all trees and grasses, many shrubs and flowers and most fruits and vegetables. At that time, the dust mite had not been discovered and I was consequently allergic to "house dust" as well. My parents were advised to get rid of our pets, remove all furniture from my room except a foam rubber mattress and pillow, instal special filters in the windows and prohibit me from eating fresh fruits and vegetables. Very fortunately, my parents considered my emotional well-being as well as my physical well-being and, although my father built filters for the windows, and I temporarily had a few dietary restrictions, they did not rid our house of pets, or indeed prevent me from touching them.

I still have allergies, and went through veterinary college with them. At university, horses caused me a little worry and during the last few years some cats with skin diseases, and some budgies, remind me of my "immune incompetence". But with these allergies I have still been able to practice veterinary medicine.

It is interesting to see how little the medical profession's attitude to allergy has changed in the three decades since I first had contact with their attitudes. Ed Baker, an American veterinarian who specialises in skin diseases of pets, and who is himself an allergic individual, actually asked them. Baker asked one hundred and seventy allergists on the East Coast what their standard recommendations were in an "allergic" household, a home in which at least one member of the family suffered from allergies. One third of these allergists said they routinely recommended removal of all pets, regardless of the problem. Some said they did so based on their experience. Others made this recommendation because it was the orthodox thing to do.

Michael McCulloch, a psychiatrist in Oregon, whose work I mentioned earlier, found in his thirties that he was developing allergies, and after he was tested, he too was advised to rid his home of all pets. "But they are part of my family," McCulloch told his allergist.

McCulloch did what Baker did and surveyed allergists on the West Coast. He found that one third refused to treat the patient if professional advice on ridding the home of pets was not followed, one third would continue treating but professed a loss of interest in the case, and one third would take the fact that the animal was part of the household into consideration and work with that fact.

The problems of allergy are presented to the veterinarian routinely and because there is never a clear answer, the veterinarian can unwittingly find himself in the position of family counsellor and decision maker. Recently, a couple came to me with such a problem. The family had bought a Yorkshire Terrier pup for their withdrawn eleven-year-old daughter. The little girl took to the pup and, as a consequence, she started to participate more in family affairs and to take on greater responsibilities. Nine months after getting the pup, the child was diagnosed as being allergic to dog dander and the family physician told them that the dog must go. The entire family accompanied the dog when they brought it to me, ostensibly because the dog was not well, but really for guidance as to what to do. Needless to say, this has nothing to do with veterinary medicine but it is still a problem that pet owners will bring to their veterinarian. It almost amounts to a request for a second opinion, and I assume that when people ask me for my advice in matters such as this, after they have been advised by their physicians, they are doing so because they are reluctant to follow their doctor's advice and want a professional opinion that is more amenable to their keeping their pets. Removing an animal from a household is an important step. It is difficult, even for the veterinarian, to appreciate the differing levels of emotional attachment that individual family members have for the pet. When I am asked my advice, I suggest doing what Michael McCulloch did, and that is to discuss the emotional complexities of removing the pet from the house with the physician or allergist. If the physician is adamant that the pet must go, there is no harm in getting another opinion. That other opinion should not come from the veterinarian but rather from another allergist.

Allergy is a physical problem caused by dogs and cats, but it is still not as great a physical problem as are bites. Many owners simply don't appreciate the potential danger that their pet represents to children, to adults, to other dogs, or even to their veterinarian. Ask any veterinarian how many times he has examined a snapping, salivating dog on the table, only to be told by the owner, "Oh, he doesn't like you", or "Nearly got you, didn't he?" or "She bites everybody." In western Canada, 14% of veterinarians have been incapacitated for at least a day because of a dog bite. And in London, when I asked my colleagues, I did not find one who had not lost at least one day's work because of dog bites.

There are over thirty-six million dogs in the United States, and until very recently there was a dramatic increase in the number of big dogs. Of the five-and-a-half million dogs in the UK in 1979, 30% were large, 38% were medium-sized and 32% were small.

Almost all statistics on dog bites show that large breeds are the greatest offenders. Figures from such disparate areas as New York City, the province of New Brunswick and South America all show that dogs over 25 kg in weight are responsible for the majority of injuries treated at hospitals. The Leeds Hospital in Yorkshire has actually quantified their costs in treating patients for dog bites, and in 1977 this was £30,000. They also calculated that the direct (police, ambulance, etc.) and indirect (lost work, etc.) cost to the Leeds Metropolitan Community in that year was £2,000,000. A number of American hospitals have reported that one in fifty visits to emergency rooms is for treatment of dog bite injuries.

Large dogs can cause such serious injuries that the injured person needs hospital treatment. But large dogs are not alone among the breeds that I think are most unreliable. My experience is that the Dachshund is as snappy as any large dog, that the Golden or Red Cocker Spaniel is the most unreliable and will bite when the owners, or passers-by, least suspect, and that the Chihuahua suffers as much as the Alsatian from nervous aggression. The difference is that these small dogs seldom cause enough damage to warrant hospitalization of the bitten.

Roger Mugford, a psychologist who treats animal behaviour problems, says that 70% of the cases he sees are problems of aggression. Victoria Voith, a psychologist and veterinarian at the University of Pennsylvania, has written that over half of the cases presented to her as a consultant in animal behaviour are problems of aggression.

Mugford has looked at the problems presented to him and has ranked the breeds in order of frequency of behavioural problems. They are as follows:

Labrador Retriever	9%	Golden Retriever	3%
German Shepherd	7%	Border Collie	3%
Cocker Spaniel	6%	Yorkshire Terrier	2%
Dachshund	4%	Old English Sheepdog	2%
Poodle	4%		

Almost half of the Labradors were brought to him because of aggression between males. But 70% of the German Shepherds were seen by Mugford because they were nervous attackers. The majority of Cocker Spaniels were presented because of unsolicited and unexpected attacks on owners and others.

If one only goes by these statistics, the impression that the German Shepherd is the only significant biter might seem valid. So Mugford and an assistant did a little dog gazing at Crufts Dog Show. They chose eight breeds of dog. Each subject first got a one minute stare from a yard's distance. Then a hand was offered, palm down, and finally the dog was stroked. Remember that these are all dogs that are used to being handled, and to get to Crufts had to have won at previous dog shows. Mugford's first interesting fact was that 57% of the smooth-haired Dachshunds had an aggressive response to the stare or proffered hand, and tried to bite. Eighty per cent of the German Shepherds huddled at the backs of their kennels and half of them showed a nervous reaction to the proffered hand. Labradors did not retreat into their kennels, but stayed up at the front. Cocker Spaniels were relaxed and at ease for both the stare and the touch.

According to these observations, the Dachshund was the snappiest dog. Veterinarians don't need statistics to tell them what to be wary of. Most of us who go on house visits know that Dachshunds enjoy ankle for afters. Robert Benchley once wrote, "Dachshunds are ideal dogs for small children, as they are already stretched and pulled to such a length that the child cannot do much harm one way or the other." To me, they suffer from the "Napoleon complex" and are always trying to compensate for having such short legs.

In Saskatoon, Saskatchewan, the areas of the city that had the poorest social and economic conditions were the areas that showed the highest incidence of dog bite injuries. If that fact is relevant to the UK, then there is an incipient problem developing here. Although the number of dogs in this country has remained static, in 1979, the last year for which there are statistics, there was a drop in pet ownership amongst the professional and managerial classes, the so-called AB group, and an equivalent increase in pet ownership in the less privileged classes, specifically the C2, D and E groups.

Dogs that live in the poorer parts of London, and especially those on large council estates, are frequently allowed to roam freely all day. They set up territory and can act like a mob of ordinary citizens, individually benign but recklessly and mindlessly destructive as a group. Some of the worst incidents of dog attacks recently have occurred when these furry skinheads have attacked as a group.

There is a breed disposition towards biting and there is an individual disposition towards biting. Individuals that are actively dominant are those that are most likely to bite. The persistent sniffers and leg-lifters are the incipient dangers. But biting is also related to the environment. Dogs bite more frequently in the summer than in winter. These bites are fair weather accidents which, in North America, reach a peak

Chihuahua suffers as much as the Alsatian from nervous aggression

during the humid "dog days" of August. Although dogs are more likely to be outdoors during fair weather, heat can probably be implicated as a factor in increased aggression. The New York City Police know that they will have more murders to contend with during humid weather, and the hospitals know that they will have more dog bite injuries to treat. Dogs that are ill and are suffering from a fever are also more liable to bite, as are dogs that are in pain or discomfort.

Male dogs bite more than female dogs, and young people under twenty years of age are those who are most frequently bitten. Most dog bites occur close to where the dog lives, implying that there is an aspect of territory defence in the biting pattern.

Above all, bites can be a problem created by the owner. They are commonly a consequence of the owner's permissive attitude towards the dog. One owner, who I will call Mick, and whose arrogance I don't find particularly appealing,

"Dachshunds are ideal dogs for small children as they are already stretched and pulled to such a length that a child cannot do much harm one way or the other."

usually arrives at the clinic without an appointment. In fact, he always arrives without an appointment. His black Labrador, Spike, barges in with him, and in a fraction of a millisecond has cocked his leg on the desk, the fireplace, various cats in baskets and clients' legs, and starts an aggressive, tail-up hackles-up confrontation with whatever is handy. Mick will reassure the other clients that "Spike is okay, I've trained him myself." But if you dare to intervene, beware of your hand. Spike is a biter because he is genetically an actively dominant dog who has never learned obedience. He's a lot like Mick.

There can be trickier and more unpleasant situations.

When I first started practising in London, I had occasion to visit a client who kept two Alsatians, Satan and Thunder. Before the owner would open the door to his house, he would shout to me to put my hands in my pockets. Only then would he open the door. Satan and Thunder would charge at me, muzzles pressed into both of my pockets. The owner would beam and say, "Aren't they beautiful? I've trained them myself." The problem was he had not trained them not to attack hands. It was impossible to get near them for any type of treatment. And he had not trained them selectively. Anytime, anywhere, hands were fair game. Gerry, the owner of Satan and Thunder, is a submissive man in all outward ways. His dogs are submissive to him but aggressive with others. They have retained their capacity to protect themselves. Their aggression is directed outward. They are loyal to Gerry, but have teeth for others. They are submissive to him not because of any powerlessness. They retain their power, but in Gerry's eyes they overcome their power (and don't bite him) because of their love for him. I would see cases such as this when I was starting practice, but I won't now. Two weeks ago I had to refuse to anaesthetize a Rottweiler that needed its ears syringed, because the owner was unwilling to handle him and I was unwilling to put my nurses at risk from an animal that was stronger than both of them combined.

Victoria Voith at the University of Pennsylvania says that most of the aggression cases she sees are directed at members of the family. In a report she presented in 1981, Voith

. . . *an aggressive tail-up,
hackles-up confrontation* . . .

recounts interviewing the mother of a three-day-old baby
that had been killed by the family dog. The dog's history was
unusual in that it lived with the family until it was 18 months
old, at which time it was given away because the woman
could not bear to see the remains of the rodents and birds that
it had killed, littering the back garden. Four years later she
found it in a kennel. It was emaciated and aggressive with
people. During those four years it had usually been kept tied
up in a back yard. Because she felt sorry for it, she brought it
home, where it played amicably with her six-year-old
daughter and with neighbourhood children.

The baby was born in hospital and brought home when it
was three days old. A few hours after they had returned
home, while the mother was standing only a few feet from
the baby and talking to her husband, the dog leapt and
grasped the baby by the head and carried it several feet away.
The dog did not show any aggression to the owners and
moved away when it was approached. The baby was taken
back to hospital and died 12 hours later.

When the mother was interviewed a week later she was coping well with her grieving and recognized both her attachment to her dog, and the horrific consequence of having that dog. The dog was taken away by the local humane society.

Yet the opposite can occur as well. Jim Van Leeuwen, a psychiatrist at the Hospital for Sick Children in Toronto, has recounted a case in which a child's nose was bitten off by the grandparent's dog. The mother of the child needed psychiatric help before she could look at the child, yet the family kept the dog.

Victoria Voith's story of the death of the baby raises the question of whether we should "recycle" dogs through dog pounds, dog shelters, dog homes and humane societies. Dogs that are abandoned are frequently abandoned because of behavioural problems, and the most common behavioural problem that specialists see is that of aggression.

Jim Van Leeuwen's story begs the question of who should decide whether a dog should be kept after a serious injury has occurred. The dog in his story had caused a terrible physical injury, deforming the child for life. The emotional injury to the mother was, in its own way, almost as bad as the physical injury, yet the grandparents kept the dog that had so damaged their family. I don't know any of the facts other than those that Dr Van Leeuwen has written. I do know that I value the emotional and physical security of children over the value of a dog or cat. Many people say that there are no bad dogs, only bad owners. The basis for that is true, but it is not a law of the universe. There are bad dogs; bad in the sense that they are unsuitable as family pets. There are some dogs that, because of breeding or simply a quirk of genes, are so aggressively dominant that only an individual who is sophisticated and experienced in dog handling should handle them. Dog lovers (or what, in the United States, are called "humaniacs") have difficulty understanding that not all dog owners have the ability to develop the empathy that they have with animals. Short of requiring all potential pet owners to pass practical examinations on their ability to cope with "difficult" dogs, we should make sure that there are as few difficult dogs as possible. Quite simply this means that dogs should be bred primarily for temperament and not, as at present, primarily for conformation and breed standards. Although many breeders do breed for temperament, it is still not the general rule. My favourite breed, the Golden Retriever, is right now in Britain being bred for certain show standards such as a broader head and peaked frontal bone, that are resulting in some nasty and snappy male Golden Retrievers. They are being bred for these features because these are the features of dogs that are winning at shows. In the show ring, temperament stands for naught.

A problem dog or cat is an animal that is unable to adapt itself to the conditions under which it must live. The feral, free-living dog or cat has a clear-cut and well-defined social environment. There are prey and predators, territorial neutrals and territorial rivals. The good family dog or cat must have the innate ability to inhibit its natural predation, to develop artificial standards for its defence mechanisms and to reduce its territorial protectiveness. Most dogs have the ability to do this, but some simply do not. The animal's ability to adapt will vary from one individual to another even within a litter, but it is, as well, something that can vary with the breed. All dog trainers know that the retriever breeds have elastic personalities and are amenable to training, but that the terriers, as a rule, are rigid and more stubborn in their ways. And most trainers will accept that there are some animals that will always be unpredictable.

A young woman recently brought her Alsatian to me for examination. The dog had been rescued by the couple from Battersea Dogs Home four months previously. It was a demonstrative and affectionate dog, but one night, for no apparent reason, it attacked the woman's husband. Several weeks later another unexpected and unprovoked attack occurred, and a month after that the woman was attacked. The dog seemed to suffer from what can only be described as a sudden avalanche of rage which was not apparently stimulated by anything happening outside the dog's body. Because the dog's whole medical history was unknown, I had to presume that this rage syndrome might be a sequel to a distemper infection before the owners bought the dog, but the problem was this. For all practical purposes, this was a dog, owned by sensible people with years of experience owning Alsatians, whose aggressive tendencies could not be anticipated. The moral dilemma that the owners faced was considerable. The woman's husband is a judge, who says that he could not carry on his duties if the death penalty were still in existence in Britain. Yet he realized the considerable damage this dog could inflict, and needed counsel on what to do. With advice from me and from an animal behaviourist, the decision was made to euthanize the dog.

The judge's Alsatian presented an unpredictable situation. There are other circumstances where breed predisposition makes everything much easier to anticipate. I know that there are some breeds, the Borzoi, the Saluki and the Afghan are three, that suffer from breed predisposed apparent depression. Their apparent depression appears when they are in hospital. They simply go off their food and starve themselves. Dogs and cats will do this too as a consequence of emotional complications in their relationships with their owners, but this can be corrected.

The animals ability to adapt will vary . . .
even within a litter

William Campbell, an ethologist, who wrote the first really sensible book on behavioural problems in dogs, has described how people, usually women, who use baby talk and constantly pet their dogs can create this type of canine emotional problem. Campbell calls this type of inadvertent dog training "pet-oriented emotional masturbation". What is happening is that an unsatisfactory emotional bond develops between owner and pet, in which each depends excessively on the other. This over pampering of pets, in fact, becomes a parody of domestication, for in its·own way it turns people into the servants of pets.

Many feelings and emotions can be displaced on to pets and cause problems for the animals, for their owners and for their veterinarians. The owners are not "abnormal" in doing so. Remember, attachment to pets increases with the length of time that you have the pet, and becomes stronger when you share happy experiences with it. It is reinforced by the animal's need for you, and by your responsibility to it. And it is reinforced each time you touch it and each time it signals with its facial movements or voice, or when you make eye contact. Your dependence upon the animal will increase if you are living alone. Attachment is normal. But the attempt to displace too much feeling or emotion on to the pet, whether because of the personality of the owner or because of particular circumstances, can be unhealthy, and this is when the problems begin.

Mrs Svenson visits the clinic regularly with her Yorkshire Terrier. Muffy is a stoic creature who is brought to me because she is supposed to be "off-colour" or off her food, or not drinking as much as she usually does, or sleeping in a different position, or a myriad of other rather nebulous signs. Almost always she is found to be exceedingly healthy. Mrs Svenson frequently asks for diagnostic laboratory work which I know to be both clinically, and financially, unnecessary. While Mrs Svenson's hyper-anxiety about Muffy may exist because of a genuine fear that something is wrong with the dog, it could also be that she might fear that she herself may have an illness and is simply transferring the signs or symptoms to her pet. Equally, Mrs Svenson may, as a large proportion of owners do, regard Muffy as a furry status

Some will actually say that they wish their vet treated people too

symbol, or "valued object", and may be acting in an extreme fashion to what she perceives as a threat to her status symbol. Owners of breeds that have a higher social status, breeds like Salukis or Burmese cats, might be more prone to feelings of great anxiety over the loss of their status symbols.

Michael McCulloch has described how some owners will use their pet as a "ticket of admission" to gain admittance for a "medical" discussion with an informed but disinterested third party. Many pet owners have great respect for their veterinarians' medical ability. Some will actually say that they wished their vet treated people too. They do so because they are impressed that we diagnose conditions without the advantage medics have of asking the patient where it hurts, or how it feels. These pet owners forget that their pets do communicate these things. It's just that they don't talk about them. I recently had a very long-standing client bring her dog in for examination, ostensibly because it was scratching itself, but in fact because she just had to talk to someone about an incident in a hospital earlier in the month. Her husband had entered hospital for elective surgery, had suffered a cardiac arrest while under anaesthesia, and had died. There had been no premonition that this might happen, and as her GP was involved, she did not want to raise the subject of a possible "mistake" with him. She was still in the "disbelief" stage of her grieving and used her pet as a "ticket of admission" to talk to me about anaesthesia and its risks.

This woman's dog was a gift to her from her husband, and it may well be that its symbolic significance will increase in the future. There is a little Border Terrier that lives around the corner from the clinic that has moved itself up several notches in significance to its owner because it started barking and came to find her when her husband suffered a stroke. But equally, pets can play a role in marital warfare.

Andrew Yoxall, when he was a faculty member at Cambridge University, corresponded with the National Marriage Guidance Council, and they had this to say about pets in marriage:

> *"Although we are not in a position to collect statistical evidence about it, I think we would support your view that relationships with pets can become entangled with relationships between spouses. We would go further and say that such confusion is probably quite common and by no means always trivial. People can invest surprising amounts of emotional energy even in inanimate possessions, and the opportunities for trying to cope with emotional problems by relating to a pet are proportionately greater. Of course, this is often done quite openly and constructively, and in general a pet can be as helpful to the maturation of a marriage as to the maturation of an individual. But where the displacement of emotion is not consciously recognised by the owner – or where it is recognized but nevertheless persistently indulged in – the owner is storing up trouble for himself and his family, and the pet is at risk of being mistreated in one way or another."*

My brother does not mind my mentioning that there was a phase in his marriage when this happened. He found himself coming home from work and saying hello to his budgie first. My sister-in-law, in turn, developed a death wish for the budgie. Their relationship and attitude to the bird was as clear an indication as any that the marriage was going through a rocky stage (which, incidentally, they were acute enough to observe, strong enough to accept, and willing enough to overcome). The budgie was a focus for their problems and for a time even made the situation worse. This is not a problem only in modern marriages. Samuel Pepys wrote in his Diary of quarrelling all night with his wife over putting their dog in the cellar because it was fouling the house.

Sometimes the pet can play a far more significant symbolic role in a marriage. In January of this year, Mr Reilly brought his Doberman dog in for me to destroy. I was interested to see him for two reasons. The first was, I had never met him. I had seen the dog possibly twenty times, but his wife had always brought it in. The other reason I was interested in seeing him was that a year previously I had arranged, and had paid on his behalf, for some fairly sophisticated surgery to be performed on one of the dog's forelimbs to eliminate a long-standing limp. Mr Reilly was my biggest bad debt.

He was in an agitated state when he came in. His hands were shaking. He looked as though he was overwhelmed with difficulties. I asked why he wanted me to destroy the animal now, after such successful surgery had been done and when the dog looked as fit as it ever did. And he told me the following. The dog was his common-law wife's dog, and Katie had always looked after him. But Katie got in a bit of trouble with the law and had disappeared, leaving him with the dog. He had looked everywhere to try to find her and bring her home, but had been unsuccessful. The dog, in the meantime, was going nuts without her. It paced back and forth and howled incessantly whenever he left the flat. It howled so much, in fact, that he could not even go out to look for a job. It was a full time job looking after the dog.

I didn't want to kill the dog because it was perfectly healthy and had had this terrific piece of surgery done on its leg. And besides, they owed me a lot of money. I asked Mr Reilly if there was any way of finding his wife. The animal's records were under her name, she had always brought the animal in and I wanted to speak to her about the situation. Mr Reilly gave me her solicitor's card. He had it in his hand. I suggested that he leave the dog with me for the next twenty-four hours and that way he could get a good night's sleep and even go out looking for a job. He thanked me and said, "All I want is for Katie to have the dog back and for me to have Katie back." We shook hands and he left for the day.

I telephoned the solicitor and told him that Mr Reilly had been in asking that the dog be destroyed. The solicitor's response was concise and clear-cut. He said, "Oh shit!" I told the solicitor that I was reluctant to kill the dog and had it in kennels at the clinic. He said "Oh double shit!" I thought to myself, "This is a man who doesn't beat around the bush", and said, "Something is going on that I should know about. What's up?" The solicitor explained very little, other than that he knew where Mrs Reilly was and would get in touch with her. He asked how Mr Reilly had behaved at my place and I said, "Fine – terrific". I said I thought the poor man was under great emotional strain and that I felt sorry for him. The solicitor asked me how I got his telephone number and I told him that Mr Reilly had given me his card. He said, "Oh shit, shit!"

That afternoon Mrs Reilly phoned, in tears. First she asked how the dog was, and I told her; then she asked how I was and I told her. Then she asked if her solicitor had told me what was happening, and I said "No". Mrs Reilly was in a hostel for battered wives.

Three weeks earlier she had escaped during a beating, but had not been able to take her dog. Since then she had been in hiding afraid that her husband was out looking for her, and more afraid that he might find her. Well, my problem was that now I had the dog. As far as I was concerned, it was hers because she had always brought it in, it was healthy and there were no indications for euthanasia, and her husband had asked me to help get the dog back to her. I asked her to come in and pick up the dog. I was looking forward to that, because I had not seen either her or her chequebook since I had paid her bill for the leg surgery. But she said she couldn't do that. She was afraid that her husband would be lying in wait outside the clinic, waiting for her to arrive. She was convinced that her husband's bringing the dog in was a ploy to find her. Instead, she said, the hostel had had a meeting; had decided first that she could keep the dog there with her, and second that two other wives would come to pick the dog up. Mrs Reilly described these women to me, and I said goodbye to her and to my ever recovering the bad debt.

I telephoned her solicitor and told him what I was proposing to do. His reply was predictable. He also said that if I were to do that, then Mr Reilly would know how Mrs Reilly got in touch with me. "Look," I said, "I'm insured for being injured by my patients, not their owners. You're the solicitor, and he's your responsibility."

Later that day, the dog was picked up, and next morning Mr Reilly returned. With a big smile, I said, "You'll never guess. Mrs Reilly got in touch and picked up the dog. You're free of it." He replied by grabbing my shirt collars and telling me he'd get me. I wouldn't know where and I wouldn't know when, but he'd get me. "You've known all along where she was," he said. "That's why you wouldn't put him down. She'd been on to you." I said that that was not the case. If I had known where she was, I would have tried to get my bad debt paid. I told him that she got in touch with me after I telephoned the solicitor. With that he was off – to the solicitor.

Pets can be used as weapons in marital problems. Mr Reilly might have been using the threat to kill something that he knew Mrs Reilly loved as a means of finding her. And it could also be argued that destroying something to which his wife was strongly attached was symbolically destroying her. Whatever the case, veterinarians will, on occasion, be asked to destroy a husband's or wife's pet by the other spouse. It is usually an indication that all is not emotionally sound in the home and the veterinarian has to be very careful that he does not fall into a marital warfare trap.

In well adjusted families, the pet (or the pets) belong to the whole family. Any major decisions are family decisions but a distinction exists between individuals who have had pets in their childhood and those who have not. Many people don't have pets, don't particularly want them and don't know how to care for them if they do end up having them. If, in a marriage, the husband and the wife have totally different animal ownership backgrounds, there is the potential for conflict. People who have been accustomed since childhood to having pets can sometimes find it difficult to understand the difficulties their partners have in understanding both the pets and their own love of the pets.

Alasdair MacDonald has said a pet can act as a substitute for several different types of attachment object, such as both a husband and a child, or may act as a fill-in for aspects of attachment behaviour that cannot be expressed elsewhere. One of the most common problems that I see is the over-indulged pet. The owners are frequently either childless or empty-nesters, and the pet is treated as a spoiled child. An even greater problem is the individual, usually a middle-aged woman, who compulsively collects animals. These people make their emotional investment completely in their animals and aside from devoting a great deal of care to them, they usually also devote the greater part of their incomes. The standard of hygiene in which these animals (and their owner) live is almost invariably low. Andrew Yoxall has written of one such situation in which cats regularly died from being "bled-out" by their massive flea burden, yet the owner, who was greatly distressed at these deaths, was either unwilling or unable to improve the situation by employing even the simplest hygiene measures.

  Because these people are emotionally totally dependent on their pets, because the bond is so strong, they will usually not permit their ill animals to be taken to hospital. What is more important, they never take holidays for fear that the animals will not be properly cared for in their absence and will refuse to enter a hospital themselves if the need arises, or move to more suitable accommodations, for fear of what will happen to their animals. Compulsive animal collectors feel that their animals can only survive and be happy through their personal intervention. They suffer from classic attachment displacement to their pets.

An even greater problem is the individual . . . who
compulsively collects animals

The smothering and over-protective care of some owners,
care that to them represents their love and concern, can
produce a neurotic dog, and then problems for the owner and
for the vet. Let me give you some examples.

Mrs Smith is in her late sixties. Her poodle is seventeen
years old, incontinent and wasting away with old age. Mrs
Smith comes in weekly for the dog to be given vitamin
injections, and each time she comes in I try to broach the
subject of the dog's miserable condition, but she refuses to be
drawn into a conversation on the subject. She lives alone and

walks with a disability which appears to me to cause her considerable pain.

Mrs Smith always appears withdrawn to me. It also seems that the only consistent relationship she still has in her life is with her very old dog. Because of that she has "humanized" that relationship and displaced on to the dog feelings of love, affection and attachment which should be shared elsewhere. The problem is that in her life there is no other place for these feelings. Mrs Smith has a very special relationship with her dog, but because of that she has put herself into a position where she will have great mental suffering when the dog dies.

Mr Jones has a Dalmatian that he shows professionally. Last year, the dog was hit by a car and required stitches in a deep gash on its hind leg. The dog was sent home wearing an Elizabethan collar so that it could not lick at the wound, but was returned to the clinic the next day with the wound wide open and not a stitch in sight. Mr Jones was fuming "Don't you know how to tie a knot?" he said. "I could have done a better job myself! Do it again, and I'm not paying you a penny more for it, and if there are any more problems I want my money back and I'm going elsewhere!" Mr Jones had, of course, taken the Elizabethan collar off the dog. He felt sorry for the animal having to wear it, but the dog, in turn, licked out all the stitches that night. And I was the butt end of the displacement of his anger at himself for doing such a thing. The pet can be the butt end of anger displacement too, and I will, occasionally, see a dog, or more usually a cat, that has been kicked by the owner when the anger was really for someone else.

Mr Brown is thirty years old, married and has never had to work in his life. He grew up in an affluent environment and lives on his investment income. Although he has two children he frequently comes into the clinic with the dog, really for a chat. The dog, a Cavalier King Charles, is a good, sensible dog. Last year, Mr Brown had an affair with a woman which, after much leniency from his wife, led to his divorce. The settlement of the divorce was uncomplicated. He gave the house to her, and custody of the children as well. His financial support for them is generous. The only oddity in the arrangement is that Mr Brown is still living with his ex-wife. He is doing so because she has the King Charles. Throughout the marriage he displaced his affection on to the dog. Now, with the abrupt change in his life, the dog's importance has increased. His displaced affection for it is still there, but the dog also now symbolically fulfils his need for roots. It is the only constant factor he has left. The fact that Mr Brown had emotional problems at home was apparent when his displaced affection for his dog increased. Compulsive care-giving to pets is as sure a sign as any that all is not well with a person's emotional attachments. The man or woman who says, "I love dogs more than people" might have been bonded to pets at an early age, but it is more likely that he or she has had disappointing relationships with other people and that the love of pets has developed as an insular reaction. In people who have normal attitudes towards pets, unsatisfactory emotional bonding with other people can result in excessive dependency upon pet animals. Prostitutes in Central London habitually keep pets. They keep large dogs for protection and care for the feral cats that inhabit their dwellings. They take better than average care of their animals and have intense, and sometimes very emotional relationships with them.

I am not saying that compulsive and over-indulgent care-giving to pets is wrong. I am just saying that it is a fact. How one chooses to look at that fact will vary with one's perspective and set of values. The compulsive care-giver often looks upon his or her veterinarian as an understanding soul; someone who understands how one can come to "love" an animal so. In these circumstances, the veterinarian may be in a position to help, simply by listening. He or she is also in a position to do harm through a lack of understanding of a situation. It is a new role for the small animal practitioner but one that several veterinary schools know exists and for which veterinarians in the future may be better prepared.

CHAPTER SEVEN

Pet behaviour and behaviour modification

In Chapter One, I briefly mentioned a few facts about the social lives of dogs and cats. I mentioned the importance of the "organization" of life for any species of animal that lives in contact and in harmony with others of its species. I also touched on the importance of play and visual communication and on how important the first twelve weeks of life are in the development of the animal's social behaviour.

An understanding of the animal's social behaviour is important if the pet is to be treated as anything other than a "quasi-human". People will say to me, "I keep telling him not to cock his leg on the curtains, but he won't listen to me", genuinely believing that a dog can understand language and vocabulary, and will respond to verbal reasoning. The dog's cocking his leg on the curtains is normal dog behaviour. It's not abnormal. It simply does not fit in with our expectations of the dog and is a behaviour which, through our training of the dog, we hope to suppress.

Cats and dogs are socialized; that is, their behaviour patterns are set, to a great extent when they are between three and twelve weeks of age. The process is so rapid in these species, compared to the socialization process in the human, that critical phases can go unnoticed.

You could say that the process of socialization begins for pups and kittens when they first tell their mothers, through sounds and movements, that they want to suckle. The play behaviour of kittens is almost completely developed by the time they are only seven weeks old, and by eight weeks of age kittens show the aggression behaviour patterns of adult cats.

Pups are the same. If they are to be socialized so that they live harmoniously with both other dogs and with people, they must have their initial contacts with both species between the third and twelfth weeks of their lives. Between six and eight weeks of age is the period of optimum socialization for pups. If they are socialized earlier than this only to people, they may become overdependent on them. And if a pup is not socialized to other dogs before it is eight weeks old – if it is taken from its litter, or in any other way denied access to other dogs – it runs the risk of developing a fear of other dogs and of showing extreme aggression to them. Male dogs that are raised like this may be impotent and females may either refuse to mate, or may be sexually attracted to people instead of dogs.

This phase of life is most critical for kittens too. If you want a cat that is comfortable in the presence of people, and happy living indoors, it must have frequent contact with people when it is between four and eight weeks of age. The kitten should be held and should be caressed frequently during this time, and preferably by different people rather than just the breeder or the owner. Michael Fox, in his book *Understanding Your Cat*, says that if a kitten has frequent exposure to different people between the ages of five and nine weeks, it will show "less fear of strangers than those handled by only one person, or not handled at all."

If kittens or pups do not have social contacts with people during this time, they may prove later to be unmanageable pets. Dogs that are socialized to people after they are fourteen weeks of age, or in some cases even twelve weeks of age, may develop shyness with humans, or the reverse, aggressiveness and dominance. For a dog to develop a balanced social response to both other dogs and to people, it is best removed from its litter when it is between six and eight weeks of age. The same applies to kittens. These animals should, barring any subsequent intentional or inadvertent abuse from humans, develop a minimum of socially unacceptable behavioural patterns.

A variety of early experiences is necessary for these young

If a kitten has frequent exposure to different people, it will show less fear of strangers . . .

animals so that they have broad social experience and mature into animals that are content both with their own species and with us. But the limits to what they can do are set by their genetic potential. Many people, for example, think that cats do not have the genetic potential to learn to perform tricks. Michael Joseph, in a book he wrote forty years ago called

Cats Company recounted performing cats exhibited by a Herr Techow; cats that were trained to walk only on their front feet, and to jump through flaming paper hoops.

Cats do not have a genetic limitation which prevents them from learning to do these things. Cat owners simply don't attempt to train their cats to do things like this. But through selective breeding and specifically in-breeding and line breeding, it is possible to produce strains of animals that are emotionally unstable and possess a narrow range of behavioural potentials. This has been done experimentally in the United States with some pointer dogs, where the researchers were able, through selective breeding, to develop neurotic dogs in a single generation. They say "the unstable line appeared as such so rapidly, and in such extreme form, that it was not necessary to make them neurotic – they developed abnormal behaviour spontaneously." These dogs were timid, had a fear of humans, reduced exploratory behaviour and an exaggeratedly startled response to loud noises. The differences between the nervous and normal animals first began to appear at around eight weeks of age. This is interesting because the "fear imprint" develops in the pup between eight and ten weeks of age. If a pup has a traumatic or fear-producing experience during this time, it may have a permanent affect and the dog may act defensively in similar circumstances in the future.

This is an important point for the veterinarian because pups are between eight and ten weeks of age when they are first brought in for their primary vaccination. If the veterinarian does not handle the situation properly, or if the owner transmits his or her fear of injections to the pup, a life-long fear of the smells and images of the veterinary clinic may ensue. People sometimes tell me, on their first visit, how clever their dogs are. "He knew I was bringing him to the vet," they say. "He started shivering as soon as we reached the front door." The dog knows where he is simply because he's had a traumatic experience in a place with similar odours once before.

Many behaviours that owners consider to be problems are not problems as far as the dog is concerned. Mick's dog, Spike, who barges into my reception room and urinates on

. . . a stratocruiser sized cat . . . launched itself from above the door

everything, is simply carrying out normal male dog marking behaviour. The dog who bites the postman is exhibiting normal canine territorial defence. These behaviours are normal to the dog, but socially unacceptable to us, and because of that we modify, or at least try to modify, them.

Cats can have socially unacceptable, but normal, behaviours too. Michael Findlay used to practice veterinary medicine in Putney, a residential area south of the Thames in London. The first, and only, time I visited his home was several years ago. Mike asked me to wait in his library while he finished seeing a client, and pointed me in the direction to take. I walked down the hall and through the door into his study. And as I did so, a stratocruiser-sized cat, screeching banzai-like sounds, launched itself from above the door onto my shoulder and started chewing. Mike came in a few seconds later, benignly grinning. "Oh, you've met my cat," he said, as I continued to swat at it. Mike's cat was not showing aggressive behaviour. It's bites were inhibited. The ambush and the mock attack were simply the normal play behaviour of an exceptionally active cat.

Dogs communicate through body postures. They say "come to me, you're my leader", or "get lost or I'll make mincemeat out of you" by subtle, or not so subtle, changes in body position. When your dog diverts his gaze from you, or when he licks you, he is showing a sign of submission. It is a

Teaching a dog to "shake hands" is a simple way for a family to establish its social dominance over the dog

passive submission, by which the dog acknowledges that he is subordinate to you. Lowering the head and neck and the ears are also signs of submission, although they should not be confused with the aggressive head lowering of the dog when he trys to protect his neck during an attack.

Your direct eye contact with your dog tells him you are dominant. If you keep it up, however, some dogs will see it as a threat and will react with fear, and perhaps try to bite.

Rolling over on his back is another way the dog tells you that you are the boss. My first Yorkshire terrier always used to greet us at the door by rolling over and "asking to be tickled". She would also bare her teeth in "a grin", and this in turn would cause her to sneeze. Both of these activities were saying, "at last, my leader has returned, welcome home. I'm yours to command." Some dogs will carry this passive submission one stage further and will urinate when they roll over to greet you. Scolding actually aggravates the problem because the dog feels submissive in the first place, and your scolding only reinforces his feeling that he is at the bottom of the pole, or lower.

Dogs that are submissive, wag their tails at the horizontal or lower. Aggressive dogs wag from horizontal up to vertical. Raising a paw is a submissive gesture, which can be used in training. Aside from teaching SIT and STAY, teaching a dog to SHAKE HANDS is a simple way for a family to establish its social dominance over the dog. Submissive dogs feel threatened when approached from above and for that reason if your dog is too submissive, it is best to get down and crouch when you greet him, and not to pat him on the top of his head, a gesture he interprets as dominant.

Aggressive dogs will signal their aggression through body posture as well. Leader type dogs show that they are dominant by physically suborning others. A leader type dog will place its forepaws on the subordinate's shoulders. In the same sense, a leader type dog will show dominance of its owner by jumping up at him or her. Jumping up, on its own, is not necessarily a display of aggression. To show aggression, the dog will carry its ears erect and its tail above the horizontal. It might also have its hackles raised, or as the behaviourists say, in piloerection. And it will probably urinate on a few scent posts to show that it means to reinforce its territorial imperative.

Dogs will signal that they are submissive by whimpering and whining, or even panting. Aggressive dogs, of course, signal their aggression with snarls and growls.

Selective breeding, however, interferes with all these signals. If holding the ears erect, the tail at the vertical and the hackles up signal that a dog is aggressive, how do you know when a bloodhound is? Rhodesian Ridgebacks are bred to look as if they permanently have their hackles up – a signal that might be considered a challenge by other dogs. Old English Sheepdogs have their tails cut off so that they cannot signal with them, their ears pendulous with the weight of hair so that they cannot be carried in an erect fashion, and their eyes covered so that, aside from not sending visual signals, you cannot even tell which end is which!

Dogs are clever psychologists. They naturally use both submissive behaviour and dominant behaviour to control situations. The little poodle that whines, scratches at the leg to be picked up, and then rolls over when it is picked up, is showing normal signs of submissive behaviour. But in doing so, it has become the owner's leader. The owner has become subordinate to the dog because, even though the dog is submissive, it is controlling the situation.

This is the central issue in any study of, or control of, pet animal behaviour. Whether they are submissive or dominant, problem dogs are leader types.

Chewing is another normal activity of dogs. The dog uses its mouth the way we use our hands. It is, aside from its nose and ability to smell, its major tool for investigation. By chewing on its littermates, the pup learns how much jaw pressure causes pain. It does the same with its owner, but if the owner allows the pup to play chewing games, and if the owner tolerates sharp bites, then the pup does not learn what constitutes play and what inflicts pain. The same applies to cats and their use of their claws. Owners who permit their kittens to climb onto their laps using claws are not giving the kittens the type of experience they need.

Pups test almost everything with their mouths, and the owner has to help the pup learn what it may and may not

If holding the ears erect, the tail at the vertical and the hackles up signal that a dog is aggressive, how do you know when a Bloodhound is?

chew. Giving the pup a box full of chewable toys is of no help. The pup will not learn to discriminate, and might chew anything. Similarly, giving it a slipper will only teach it that all shoes are chewable. Toys made of cloth or leather should be avoided, and instead the pup should be given one or two chewable articles and should be reprimanded when it chews anything else. Games like tug of war should also be avoided, because these focus on the mouth and make the dog more orally oriented. Some pups are simply more oral than others and will relieve tension by chewing. The owners always tell me that their pets are getting back at them for being left alone. They are not! Dogs are not showing spite when they chew things after they have been left alone. They are just relieving tension. Dogs are great tension relievers; far better than we are. They chew things, suck and lick themselves, dig or scratch, pace or jump. They bark and whine, and all these things are done to relieve tension. They relieve their own tension, but only increase that of their owners.

Dogs are unusual because they can form such strong social attachments to people. The owner's presence or absence can have a profound influence on the dog. Owners, although they are usually unaware of it, send a steady stream of comfort signals to their pets. The half-hearted slap, or "naughty boy", can actually be rewarding to the dog. Owners are always reinforcing both good *and* bad behaviour. The average pet owner, in fact the average veterinarian, has little understanding of the complex social nature of pack animals like dogs, and to a lesser extent cats. We will know more once people like Victoria Voith and Roger Mugford write books on the subject, and these books enter the veterinary student's curriculum.

A dog or a cat behaves the way it does because, as a result of the experiences it has early in its life, it develops conditioned

Giving the pup a box full of chewable toys is of no help

responses to certain situations. If these situations or experiences are repeated on a daily basis, the reflex response becomes clocked into the dog's behaviour. My dog is fed at 5.45 each afternoon. If she is not fed at 5.45, she searches me out and stares me down. Similarly, Honey goes on my house visits with me, and these are always made at lunchtime. Car rides are a highlight of her life, probably because she knows that they always involve a stop in Hyde Park. Whether or not I have visits to make, and regardless of whether she has been sleeping soundly upstairs, or lying by my desk, at twelve noon she gets up, shakes herself and gives me her "alert" look. She does this because it has become a conditioned reflex clocked into her mental functioning.

Just as Honey has been conditioned to respond to car rides, she has also been conditioned to the sound of words. The word "park", combined with the car journey, resulted in her alert attentiveness, but it did not take long before we only had to say the word "park" for her to be at the door waiting to go. She was conditioned to respond to the sound of the

A dog or a cat behaves the way it does because it develops conditioned reflexes to certain situations

. . . the next time the dog thinks you are going to stand on his tail, it might bite you again

word. This is what we do when we train dogs to respond to words like "sit" and "stay". Initially, we couple the verbal command with a food or affection reward, but once we have trained the dog to "sit" or "stay", we can produce a reflex response to the verbal command alone.

This is how many problems are created as well. If your dog is of the excitable type and you accidentally stand on its tail, its instinctive, rather than conditioned, response is to bite. The next time the dog *thinks* that you are going to stand on its tail, it might bite you again.

Most behaviour problems have their origins when dogs are between four and twelve weeks of age. During this time, the pup has to learn to control or inhibit its basic instinctive reflexes in order to live harmoniously with people. William Campbell lists the following as the innate instinctive reflexes that the dog must learn to control. When you read them you might agree with Campbell that city living is the absolute opposite of the type of environment that would be ideal for a dog's serene behavioural development.

The dog has an innate "freedom" reflex and will resist physical force, threats or constraints upon its freedom. Its "defence" reflex will cause it to try either to escape from a threatening situation, to freeze, or to fight. Campbell says that the threat need not only be a physical threat; any threat to social or territorial relationships can stimulate the defence reflex just as well. The third reflex is alimentary. Dogs naturally eliminate after eating, drinking, awakening, after excitement and after chewing and sniffing. Dogs also have orienting and investigating reflexes which cause them to investigate by chewing or tasting, or sniffing or even pawing things that are novel and unknown. And finally, dogs have a reflex to chase things.

All of these are natural and instinctive reflexes. They need to be modified so that the dog fits into our environment without running away from it, or biting or threatening us, or indeed chewing our possessions or urinating on our belongings.

In conditioning dogs, we stimulate them to perform certain actions and reward them for doing so. But if that dog is a leader type, look at what happens. The dog comes over and nudges the owner. The owner pets the dog. The dog stops nudging the owner. Stimulus, response and reward. But it's backwards. The dog is training the owner! It may seem silly, but the dogs I treat train their owners as much, or more, than the owners train their dogs. This, naturally, depends on the owners' attitude to their pets. People who endow their pets with emotional and intellectual capacities which are unique to the human, consistently misinterpret their pets' behaviour and are prone to being trained by them. People who want their dog's love and loyalty run the same risk. Most people do, and that is why there are so many problem dogs.

The way people treat their pets, combined with the pets' genetic predisposition, very often results in the dog assuming a leadership role with one or several members of the family. Remember, the dog does not have to be dominant to be a leader. It can use submissiveness to gain control of its family. A leader type dog may be unaggressive towards the family but aggressive with strangers. If it is dominant, it might demand the leader's right to sleep where it pleases, and may growl when forced, or just asked, to leave the owner's bed. Dogs will jockey themselves into the best possible position they can find. Many owners don't realize what is happening, and slowly and insidiously become their dogs' followers, rather than remaining the leader.

Pet owners should look upon proper pet behaviour as being as important as proper health care. Many more people are doing so now, and that is why there are now pet animal behaviour specialists working in the United States and in Britain.

The line between medical disease and behavioural abnormality can be fuzzy, however. Is a cat urinating on the carpets because it is upset at a change in its life-style or because it has a bladder infection? Is a bitch snapping at children because it is developing a conditioned aggression towards children, or because of the hormonal changes of its being in heat? Is a dog obsessively licking its forepaw because it is frustrated and bored, or because it has a deep and chronic infection?

These questions must first be answered by the veterinarian. A dog's or cat's behavioural changes can be caused by pain or a fever. Cortisone treatment is said to increase the aggressiveness of dogs. Some types of epilepsy are so unusual (like fly-catching non-existent flies) that they are easily

. . . assuming a leadership role with one or several members of the family

mistaken for behavioural problems. And problems as disparate as lead poisoning and inherited blood sugar deficiency can affect a dog's or cat's behaviour. If a behavioural problem is going to be treated, the first step must be to eliminate any physical or organic cause of the behaviour. Once these causes have been eliminated, then proper diagnosis of the behavioural problem should be made and modification techniques can be employed.

The dog's or cat's ability to respond to behaviour modification depends on that animal's internal response threshold. Much more, it depends on the owner's willingness to carry through the necessary retraining that will modify a particular behaviour.

The basis for retraining involves several of the following. You ignore the behaviour that you don't wish the dog to carry out. You redirect the dog's energy elsewhere and retrain it to carry out some other acceptable behaviour. And you punish the dog when it continues to perform the unpleasant or unacceptable behaviour.

The theory is simple, but the practice can be exasperatingly difficult. Each summer my family spends the month of August at the cottage where I grew up in the Kawartha Lakes in Ontario. Nearby, on Stoney lake, friends have Tiffany, a spayed Springer Spaniel, with an obsession for retrieving games especially games that involve water. Tiffany lives for the summer, and visitors are greeted with a stick or little log, dropped at their feet. Almost inevitably, the visitor gives in and throws the stick, but doing that simply opens the floodgate. Tiffany is yours for the day and will trail you and pester you until you leave. Tiff does not care what she has to do to retrieve a stick. She will sail through the air off a ten-foot precipice and then swim and search for half an hour until she recovers her prize. Each summer, although perfectly well fed, she reduces her body to skin and bones, simply by using up so much energy.

If we were to apply behaviour modification principles to Tiffany, this is what we would do. First, the owners would have to tell all visitors simply to ignore Tiffany's proffering of articles to be used for retrieving. Tiffany quite simply puts visitors under a benign siege. The best thing to do would be to put a distance between you and Tiffany; to walk away. Grabbing her if she follows does not help. Tiff would just interpret that as a bit of a game.

Tiffany is bursting with energy and must use it some-where, so one thing we could do is redirect her energy into an activity that we feel is more appropriate. We could play tug of war, or go jogging with her. The problem is that fetching games are so extraordinarily fascinating to her that it would be almost impossible to redirect her energies else-where.

We could punish her for persisting in her demands to play retrieving games. Punishment need not be physically painful, but it must be strong enough or forceful enough to stop the behaviour pattern of which we do not approve. A simple smack with a rolled newspaper, or a stern "no" might be sufficient. Roger Mugford, an animal behaviourist, frequent-ly arms his clients with water pistols. A quick shot between the eyes when the dog is engaging in the undesirable behaviour can be an effective punishment. Some American animal behaviourists use an ultrasonic device that can emit an uncomfortable sound wave whenever it is pressed. The most important thing about punishment is that it should not be so strong that it produces anxiety, or an aggressive response from the dog.

The punishment must be perfectly timed. Punishment must be meted out while the dog is actually engaged in the undesirable behaviour. And it must be carried out every time the dog does what you are trying to eliminate. Most pet owners can't do this, and certainly in Tiffany's case it would be difficult to convince all visitors to discipline her when they were offered sticks. Occasional punishment, or punishment too long after Tiffany has engaged in the behaviour, will be of no value. Tiffany will be saying to herself "They smack me about one out of every ten times I do this, but Jeez, I just love this game so I'll take my chances and continue."

Finally, we can counter condition Tiffany to do something which is incompatible with retrieving games. The basis for any counter conditioning is to teach the dog to "sit" and "stay". If that is not done, or if the owners do not have the ability or desire to do it, it will probably be impossible to retrain the dog. In order to retrain the dog, the owners must be convinced that it is necessary to do so, and committed to carry out the retraining. Victoria Voith, a veterinarian and a psychologist at the University of Pennsylvania, has a succinct sign in her office. It says: "SIT – STAY – DR. VOITH WILL BE WITH YOU SHORTLY!" She should have the sign. I gave it to her.

In order to counter condition Tiffany, we could utilize the fact that she already responds to sit-stay. Each day, we could spend a few minutes teaching her an alternative behaviour. The behaviour must be one that involves activity because Tiffany is an animal who needs a lot of activity. Once she has learned the new activity, be it backwards somersaults or walking only on her hind legs, we should get her to perform that activity before she has a chance to perform the one we are trying to eliminate. If it were possible, we should remove all the items she might use in retrieving games, but in the woods and rocky shores around Stoney Lake, that is, naturally, impossible. Finally, we should reward Tiffany, with either food or affection, when she greets visitors and does not demand that they participate in retrieving games.

Counter conditioning alone will not eliminate Tiffany's pestering of visitors for them to play retrieving games with her but it will help.

A cat's behaviour can be modified in almost the same way. The punishments that are used with cats are almost the same as those used for dogs. Loud vocal commands, swats on the rump with a rolled-up newspaper, and the handy water pistol are all punishing to cats. They should always be coupled with an angry "No". Roger Mugford also suggests throwing something like a shoe, not at, but beside, a cat when it is engaging in a behaviour that the owner finds unpleasant. In other words, startle the cat.

The cat's activity should be redirected elsewhere, and it should be counter conditioned into an activity which is incompatible with the unpleasant behaviour.

The most important point, as with dogs, is to have a consistent and stringent programme of reinforcing the cat's appropriate behaviour while punishing its inappropriate

behaviour. Any sensible cat, if given the choice of punishment
or reward, will choose reward. The problem for the owner
is, you have to catch the cat being good.

Many owners find the rigours of behaviour training impossible. After all, they bought their pets in the first place for
their contact comfort and emotional support. To withdraw
selectively their social contact from their dogs and cats, to pet
them only as a reward, is well nigh impossible. Praising and
petting are the greatest comfort signals that you can give to
social animals like dogs and cats, and in the initial training or
subsequent retraining of a pet, must be used sparingly. With
this in mind, there are several things that the owner should
do with a new pup.

The move from its litter, perhaps through a pet-shop, into
a person's home has to be one of the most traumatic
experiences a pup or kitten will ever have. The owners
should be aware of this and should be prepared for the
problems that may ensue. One of the most important points
to remember is that pups usually go through this process
when they are eight to ten weeks old. This is the fear-imprint
period in a pup's life. The way a pup is handled at this time
will have an effect on its long-term behaviour.

Pups will whine when they need physical comfort, but a
lot of coddling in response will only condition the pup to use
whining as a tool to attract attention later in life. Whining
should not be punished, because it is a call for comfort.
Owners should pick up the pup when it whines. That way, it
gets comfort, but at the same time the owner demonstrates
dominance. The pup should not be carried about all day, but
rather should only be held for a few minutes at a time.

The sleeping arrangements for the pup are terribly important. If you remember that it has been with its mother and
litter mates all its life, and if you remember that it is a social
animal and needs contact comfort as much as you do, then it
becomes obvious that the pup will whine and cry if it is left in
the kitchen, for example, each night. Leaving it alone will
almost always result in whining and barking, and if you do
leave it alone now, you might be laying the foundation for
fear of isolation, and in turn the tension-relieving destructive
problems that so many owners have to contend with.

The best solution that animal behaviourists have found, on both sides of the Atlantic, is for the pup initially to sleep in its own bed in someone's bedroom. An enclosed "den" can be made from an overturned cardboard carton with a doorway cut through. This can be placed over the pup's bed. Little dogs can be trained to sleep in their travelling cases. This has the added advantage of conditioning them to like the travelling case and not to go nutty later on in life because they associate it with a trip to the veterinary clinic or a stomach-wrenching car journey.

The floor of the bedroom should be covered with newspaper. Most pups will sleep through the night, but the additional advantage of having the pup sleep in the bedroom is that first thing in the morning it can be taken to the spot

The sleeping arrangements for the pet are terribly important

where you want it to urinate and defecate. When the pup performs its functions in the place where you want it to, reward it with praise and affection. Pups will need to urinate or defecate after food, after sleeping, after exercise or after a good sniff. These are the times to take the pup to its toilet area. Sticking the animal's nose into its urine is useless and only makes for problems in the future. If any discipline is given, it is only valuable if given while the pup is actually in

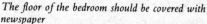

The floor of the bedroom should be covered with newspaper

the process of urinating and defacting. A firm "no" and temporary withdrawal of social contact is in order. It is much more important to reward good behaviour.

Avoid tug of war games at this age. The pup will only generalize to other things and can become a chewer. And avoid over-exciting the pup through too much play or emotional displays, for these can predispose the pup to have these behavioural qualities when he is older.

The pup's teaching sessions should be no longer than a few minutes at a time, and should always end with a reward such as lavish praise and petting. If the owner restricts petting only to these occasions, the pup will soon learn that it must earn its reward from its "leader". It is naturally most important that the pup looks upon all family members as leaders.

Subordinate or follower dogs, to quote William Campbell "do not violate (chew) their leader's belongings, steal their food, or soil their property (house)."

The most important behaviour to teach the pup is to respond to the command SIT. The owner should say the pup's name, followed by the word "Sit". If a hand is held above but just behind the pup's head, it will naturally sit, just to keep watching the hand. A food reward and praise should be given each time this is done and it will only take a dozen or so commands before the pup will sit without the hand signal.

The owner's objective in his or her relationship with the pup should initially be to develop and maintain a position of leadership. The problem dogs I see are, either through dominance or submission, acting as initiators of behaviour in their owners. They are taking the position of leadership. There are a number of things that an owner can do to maintain a leadership position with pets. Victoria Voith has suggested the following:

1. Never ask a dog to do something unless it is predicted the pet will obey, or someone is in a position to make it obey (i.e. do not ask a dog to "come" unless it is on a lead and can be made to come).
2. Do not let the dog get into a situation where it is likely to misbehave and will not obey.
3. Practice obedience tasks and parlour tricks routinely.
4. Rarely give the dog anything for free (i.e. before the dog is fed, make it sit; before it is petted, make it sit; before it is allowed onto a lap, make it sit).
5. Occasionally take an object or food away from the dog, praise it for being non-aggressive and then return the object.
6. Occasionally remove the dog from its resting place and praise it for willingly complying.
7. Periodically restrain the dog in some way for a few minutes.
8. Frequently groom the dog.
9. Occasionally hold the dog's muzzle closed by hand for a few seconds, or push the dog over on its side

and hold it there temporarily. If it does not naturally elevate its leg when this is done, lift the leg into the submissive position.

10. Frequently look directly at the dog until it looks away.
11. On occasion, gently pull the dog by its ruff or, if it is little, pick it up.
12. Do not allow the dog to demand attention by either pawing or barking, or by placing its forepaws on a person.

Frequently groom the dog

Both Roger Mugford and Victoria Voith have compiled statistics on the behavioural problems with which they are presented, and psychological and behavioural profiles of the owners of these animals. Dr Mugford has found no psychological trait that distinguishes people with problem pets from other pet owners. Nor does Dr Voith. She says, "The people themselves appear to be quite normal; no apparent neuroses, psychoses or idiosyncracies. If anything, my clients seem to be better educated, more intelligent and rational than the average owner I see across the table as a regular practicing veterinarian." Both of them say that many of these people have previously taken their pets to obedience control classes. Dr Mugford writes that roughly one-third have excellent obedience control of their pets, one-third have moderate control and one-third have poor control. These psychologists concluded that the techniques and authority obtained during standard obedience training do not necessarily transfer to the home environment where most of the behavioural problems occur.

People will keep their pets even under extreme circumstances. Roger Mugford has told me of one incident in southwest England in which a Dachshund tore open its owner's jugular vein, yet the owner kept the dog.

Dr Voith has asked her clients why they have not got rid of their pets because of the behaviour problems. Fifty-five per cent mentioned their affection for the pet as their reason for not doing so. Sixteen per cent responded with the second most frequent reason, humanitarian considerations. They gave answers like, "I feel that people have a responsibility to a pet", or "No-one else would take this animal". Others say that the animal has positive attributes that outweight the negative qualities of the behaviour problem, or simply that the pet is "a member of the family" and, as such, not in a position for the owners to contemplate removing it from the home.

Both American and British surveys consistently show that the majority of cases seen by animal behaviourists are those involving aggression. Dogs and cats can exhibit many types of aggression – territorial, predatory, sexual, maternal, irritable and fearful.

Many of the problems concern aggression within the home. When I worked in San Francisco, my boss's daughter, then four years old, went to a free school. "Free" meant freedom of expression. One day, Tara came home, into the office, and started climbing up onto the table while her father was examining a dog. "Please don't climb up on the table, Tara," her father said, "Daddy is examining a dog." "Fuck you, daddy," she replied. That is the way many dogs treat their owners. Sparkie, a four-year-old male, neutered Dachshund, does so in his home. Sparkie has bitten Mr Trani's nose. Unfortunately, Mrs Trani, who openly accepts that the dog is a child substitute, fell about laughing. When Sparkie bites Mr. Trani, he responds by shouting and hitting the dog, but Sparkie only comes back for more. Pain to Sparkie only increases his dominance aggression.

Sparkie has never been a problem to me in the clinic, nor to my staff, and Mrs Trani says that he is never a problem out of doors, only in the home, and especially with her husband. This dog, simply because it is a Dachshund, has a constitutional predisposition to aggression, but it is the owners' treatment of him that has created a monster. It's aggression is possessive of Mrs Trani, in the manner of a thoroughly spoilt child. Sparkie lives by the old proverb "the worst dog gets the best bone". The dog snaps and snarls at Mr Trani only when Mrs Trani is present. In its home it will also snap and snarl at anyone else if they try to see her. The problem is so acute that Mrs Trani's friends no longer visit her.

I asked Roger Mugford to visit Mrs Trani so that he could evaluate the situation and offer advice. Dr Mugford rang her intercom bell, introduced himself and was instructed to push the door open and to bring in the fire screen that was sitting outside the door. This was not simply errantly left outside her front door. It was for Dr Mugford's protection. He entered the house, fending off Sparkie with the fire-screen, and went to the living room. The house was full of teddy bears for the dog, another manifestation of the fact that the dog was a child substitute. Dr Mugford spent the evening with Mr & Mrs Trani, and with Sparkie, and made his observations. Sparkie had a real galloping dominance problem. I think it is worth reading Dr Mugford's letter to Mrs

The house was full of teddy bears for the dog, another manifestation of the fact that the dog was a child substitute

Trani in full. The dog was set on breaking up the Trani's marriage, and this was the advice she was given:

"*Dear Mr and Mrs Trani,*

Re SPARKIE

"*Following my visit on 9th April, I am writing to reiterate my advice and assessment of Sparkie's behaviour. He presents a dramatic example of a dominating and thoroughly spoilt smooth-haired dachshund. There are strong constitutional elements to some of the aggressive behaviours which he presents, but I am sure that your own reactions have tended to exacerbate the problems. Indeed, you occupy a very uncomfortable behavioural trap. The outlook for resolving these problems is that it will not be easy, and we have no option but to apply the strategy outlined below in a determined fashion and as quickly as possible. Thus, I recommend the following:*

1. *Mrs Trani in particular must increase her dominance over Sparkie, rejecting him on all occasions when it is he that initiates behavioural sequences. Treat him like a dog, and*

deprive him of rights and privileges, such as coming onto chairs and knees. You must be tough and only show love or affection in response to his presenting submissive behaviour patterns. He must on all occasions believe that when you give a command it is meant. Do not interact with him conversationally but rather as though he were a very junior member of an army regiment. However, I would not recommend that anyone was physical in punishing Sparkie.

2. If Mrs Trani has a cooler relationship with Sparkie, he will be less protective towards her and more friendly towards Mr Trani, other members of the family and your friends. Thus, do not allow him to continue this very flattering habit of being protectively aggressive with Mrs Trani.

3. Sparkie's aggression towards visitors is downright anti-social and could lead to a very unpleasant lawsuit. The routine outlined in the leaflet I left with you applies. A trailing lead attached to a stout collar, dominant commands to SIT–STAY by the two of you, visitors offering titbits and friendship, letting him come forward to investigate them when it is safe to do so, all apply. Thereafter, allow only friendship but no dominance from visitors, but dominance and coolness from both of you.

4. Because Sparkie is now such a dangerous dog, I would strongly advocate that you consult Dr. Fogle about a hormone treatment for Sparkie which should reduce the short-term risks of his aggression. Be advised by him on the dose and duration.

5. Within a week or two of receiving this, and having commenced the hormone treatment, contact me again for a second visit. We should review progress and continuing problems.

I well understand why Sparkie is loved, and indeed he presents very many attractive traits. However, past bite incidents are a warning that urgent action is required. Be in touch with news of progress, and ask for further help if it is needed."

Yours sincerely,
Dr. R. A. Mugford"

Dogs can also be aggressive with other dogs. This is the most common reason why owners of male Labradors ask Dr Mugford for advice. In one British survey, 30% of owners of intact male dogs said that their dogs fought with other males. A dog may be perfectly friendly with the family and congenial with strangers, but a real beast with other dogs.

Leslie Ann Down, and her sister Angela, took on the responsibility for looking after Jack, their neighbour's male German Shepherd, after their neighbour died. Miss Down's Great Dane, Oscar, a typically placid male, was quite amenable to the situation until Jack started engaging in very dominant play with him. Jack would tease Oscar and provoke him, and although Oscar was a placid dog, he would only stand for so much and would finally respond physically, with a bloody fight ensuing. What was worse for Miss Down was that Oscar's response was becoming generalized and he was becoming irritable with other dogs as well.

Jack was provoking Oscar because he wanted to jockey himself into a stronger and more important position with his leader, his leader being either of the Misses Down or whoever was responsible for exercising the dogs.

In a situation such as this, the owner has to display strong dominance and leadership over the aggressor. Jack was punished each time he teased Oscar, by being isolated from his leader in a "sit-stay" manner, while the dog walker continued to interact with Oscar. The Downs were very good at this. In return for his compliance, Jack was given a food reward. They also eliminated shows of affection for Jack both before and after walks, but increased their play with both dogs during the walks and rewarded Jack with praise and affection when he behaved with Oscar in an acceptable way, showing normal tolerance of him. Jack's aggressive displays were under control in a few weeks.

In this relationship, although he was smaller and only a recent arrival in the home, Jack the German Shepherd had taken on the leadership role over Oscar the Great Dane. But in the meantime, Oscar, in turn, had developed an aggressiveness with other dogs and this was the second part of the problem that had to be overcome.

Overcoming this type of aggression can be a slow process

for which you need some pet-owning friends who are willing to help out. The first stage is to practice sit-stays for around a week, teaching the dog to anticipate a food reward for a correct response. In the next week, the Downs practiced the sit-stays in the presence of a female dog, while Oscar was out exercising and not on his own territory. Oscar was kept on a retractable lead that allowed him to roam up to 20 feet away but to be still on line for discipline and control. A friendly female dog, especially one that is known to the aggressor, is the least likely to provoke aggression. Once the aggressor has practiced his sit-stays with food rewards in the presence of the friendly female, the distance between them is gradually reduced until, in the ultimate situation, the aggressor no longer shows aggression. The same routine can be applied using the breed or sex or colour of dog that provokes the most aggressive response. If the aggressor persists in making threats during this training, he should be grasped by the back of the neck and given a slight shake. Severe punishment can possibly intensify the aggression. The dog might associate the punishment with the presence of the other dog.

A final type of obvious aggressiveness, the one that the veterinarian likes least, is self-protective aggression. These are the dogs that growl when they are scolded and try to remove the veterinarian's hands when they are touched. The self-protective dog is physically assertive and active. It is a leader-type and will look you straight in the eye. Just saying its name can cause it to raise its hackles, cock its leg and lower its head. William Campbell has recounted a Doberman that was self-protectively aggressive. This dog was particularly protective of his rump. If the owners merely touched his hind end, the dog would freeze, turn to the rear and growl aggressively. The owners, of course, would back off, only reinforcing the dog's behaviour.

Campbell says that this type of dog responds best to what he calls the Jolly Routine. Vocally soothing jollies are given with the objective of getting the dog to wag his tail and act in a happy manner. On the occasion that Campbell describes, he explained all of this to the veterinarian; that the dog would accept physical manipulation as long as the manipulator laughed a lot while undertaking the examination. A rear-end examination was necessary on this dog because of a possibly inflamed prostate gland, and so, on the next visit, the veterinarian hopped out from behind his examining table, "ho-ho-ho-ing" like a demented Santa Claus, and almost lost his hand. Let me tell you, I understand how he felt. There is nothing particularly funny about being threatened by a large dog. The mistake that he made was to surprise the dog. Once the surprise was overcome, the Doberman did allow the prostate examination.

I try to deflect the dog's attention from what can be an uncomfortable procedure in a number of ways. First of all, I put some local anaesthetic ointment on the glove that I will use for the internal examination. Then I don't jack the tail up but leave it in as natural a position as possible. In the meantime, I have the owner offer some titbits to the dog, and with my free hand I either tickle his ear, or lightly slap him on the shoulder. All of this is done to distract his attention and make the episode as unmemorable as possible.

The over-enthusiastic watch dog manifests his aggressiveness through the defence of his territory. I see one of these in its own home every month or so when I have lunch with its owner. Julia is a wire-haired Dachshund. She is a terrific little dog, once you are in the flat and settled down. But she goes berserk with barking when the door bell rings, and will chew your ankle if given a chance. Her owner responds as most people do to their vigorously barking dogs. Julia is simply picked up and scolded when she barks, and then banished to the bedroom. Once the visitor is in, Julia is allowed back into the lounge, but there she is either held or stroked by her owner.

Julia has won, because she has got the contact with her owner and prominance of importance that she was after; but not only has she won, her aggressive reactions have also been reinforced. As far as Julia is concerned, if she barks and acts aggressively, she gets an emotional reward.

If Julia were to be retrained, she would first have to be taught her sit-stays. Once that was done, any aggressive reaction to the doorbell ringing would be coupled to a "sit" command (and the command enforced) before the visitor would be allowed to enter. In the meantime, the owner would have left some titbits outside the front door, and having been instructed as to what to do, the visitor would offer them to the dog. It would be best for the visitor to avoid eye contact with Julia because she might interpret this as aggression towards her. Julia should not be excluded physically when a visitor comes into the flat, but she should be excluded socially by her owner, yet petted by the visitor. This is probably the most important thing to do. If Julia's owners act coldly towards her, she is forced to seek her social contact from the visitors.

The dog is, socially speaking, never permanently at rest. Many fit into the American dream because they are always looking for opportunities to move up the social scale. Male dogs, or neuters, are more likely to be upwardly mobile, but the change in a dog's social status can result in a lack of obedience and physical aggression.

"Bomber" Malone saved his family from a fire. He is a five-year-old male black Labrador who, smelling smoke one night in his owner's Lisson Grove council house, ran into each room, awakened the parents and teenage children, and in doing so enabled them to get out of the flat, still in their bed clothes but before the entire house was consumed by flames.

The story is suitable for a brave dog award from the Royal Society for the Prevention of Cruelty to Animals. But there is a flaw. Bomber was naturally treated like a hero by the family. Love and affection was poured upon him, and no food was too good for him to eat. Bomber saw his opening. His owners were treating him as their leader, so he decided to move up the scale and take on that position. He started behaving aggressively with the children, and soon he had moved up three positions, to just below the parents themselves. That is when the Malones brought him in to see me. They thought that his behaviour change was the result of some brain damage because of smoke inhalation. It was not, of course. It was just Bomber moving his way up the pecking order.

Bomber's obedience problem and aggression with the children was exacerbated by the general chaos which followed the fire. Westminster Council put the family into a fourth floor flat in a tenement-like block while their house was being rebuilt, and this unsuitable and unstimulating environment for an active, large dog only increased the problem.

I asked Roger Mugford for his advice, and he visited the family and described a suitable series of training procedures for them to follow. Unfortunately, they did not find it possible to do so, and Bomber continued his aggressive ways. Finally, Bomber the hero, the dog who saved the entire family from death, was given away. The saddest aspect of the story was that his saving them was ultimately the reason that they had to rid themselves of him.

After aggression, the second most common problem that both Victoria Voith and Roger Mugford are presented with is that of separation or isolation anxiety. Almost one quarter of the cases that Dr Mugford sees involve isolation anxiety. Dogs show their anxiety by being destructive or barking or urinating and defecating in the home.

Separation anxiety is a behavioural problem created inadvertently in the pet by its owners. It is unwittingly encouraged by owners who stroke and pet their dogs when they whine, but who do not reward silence and relaxation in a similar fashion.

Jackson McLeod is a classic example of the under stimulated but over excitable London house dog, who uses destructiveness and howling to obtain social contact with his human family. Jackson is an eight-year-old male Cocker Spaniel who lives in a luxurious jail. Most London house dogs, when you consider how they are treated, live in jails. They may be comfortable and well fed. They may be given all the affection they need, and more, but for their entire lives they are released from jail once or twice a day, for a little social activity and exercise in the park, only to be returned home and locked up again. The London house dog is an under stimulated creature who frequently develops neuroses and works out the frustration of boredom by being destructive or by howling.

Jackson did just that whenever he was left alone. He would go into the kitchen, open as many drawers as he could, and

chew anything made of wood, leaving a shredded pile of splinters. He would pull the bedspread off the bed and throw cushions off the sofa. The amount of damage that Jackson could perpetrate in an evening was quite spectacular.

As in all other situations, modification of his behaviour had to start with teaching Jackson to sit-stay. The second preliminary step was teaching the owners to use what Roger Mugford calls the dominance hold. To show dominance and leadership over the animal, you straddle it and put your arms around its chest. I usually tell people to lift ever so slightly so that the front legs are temporarily no longer bearing weight.

With these procedures having been mastered, the proper behaviour modification training can begin.

Jackson's owners were instructed to stop all casual petting of Jackson, and they were told to ask their visitors to do likewise. The dog was simply ignored. This was most important just before leaving Jackson alone. He was to have no comfort before a departure. The McLeods then started making mock departures, at first returning almost immediately and praising Jackson for being quiet and nondestructive, and then for longer periods. The length of time of the mock departures did not increase uniformly. If that were done, Jackson would have been trained into a specific pattern. Instead, the McLeods departed for five minutes, then ten, fifteen, ten, fifteen, five, etc., always rewarding Jackson if, upon their return, he was quiet and had not been destructive. If he was either noisy or destructive, he was punished with the dominance hold and social ostracism.

The McLeods also accustomed Jackson to being alone when they were at home, by shutting him in the kitchen for frequent periods and rewarding his quietness and punishing unruliness. They also provided him with a rawhide toy. On one occasion, they actually threw water on him after he had misbehaved. Both of the owners work, but they were fortunate in that one of their employees, Mr McLeod's chauffeur, was willing to spend extra time exercising the dog, and this was the final step in Jackson's behaviour modification. He was taught retrieving games and, as a consequence, uses up a little more of his pent up energy each time he is exercised.

Jackson's frustration at being isolated and separated from his human family resulted in a neurotic response. Dogs can insidiously develop neuroses. Frequently, the owners look upon their pets' quirky behaviour as doggy eccentricity, and initially find it funny. I usually find it funny too, but after a while the neurosis becomes a bore, and finally a burden.

I know of one miniature Dachshund that bites his owner's ankle each time she starts playing her piano. As the owner is a professional concert pianist, it is a bit of a problem. The neurosis started about a year previously. Heinz would growl menacingly whenever his owner played Elgar. The growl developed into a lip-raised snarl, and finally an attack on her feet as they moved on the pedals. The owner has not modified Heinz's behaviour. She simply locks him in another room whenever she practices. Most owners of small dogs would probably opt for that alternative. It avoids the onerous task of repetitive retraining.

The most common problem that cat owners bring to behaviourists is what the behaviourists call "inappropriate elimination". That means urinating in the sink or defecating on the sofa. In order to alter this, it is important to understand normal elimination behaviour in cats.

House cats that have returned to the wild often use the same places repeatedly to urinate and defecate. They do not cover their droppings with dirt as house cats do, but instead leave them exposed, as dogs do, as territorial markers. They do not deposit one batch directly on top of another batch. A tom cat, scenting a female in season, will spray urine on all sorts of things within its territory and will leave its droppings throughout the area. This cat is using its urine and faeces as a form of sexual communication. Even if the tom cat has been castrated, there is still the possibility that he will scent mark an area. This is most likely to occur in the spring. Cats are most active sexually at that time of year. Increasing light entering the eyes triggers chemical changes in the brain which, in turn, stimulate the pituitary gland to release hormones that stimulate changes in the ovaries or testes. Castrating a cat only affects the final stage of that pathway, and that is why some neutered females will still "call" and why some neutered males will still spray.

Controlling urination and defecation is not, then simply controlling biological waste. By placing controls on a cat's elimination behaviour, the owner is also placing a control on a form of communication. With this in mind, if a litter box is going to be successful it should be emptied of droppings daily. Cats in the wild prefer relatively clean areas for elimination, and leaving a litter box dirty is almost an invitation for the cat to leave its droppings behind a table or under a bed. Likewise, if there is more than one cat, each cat should have its own litter box. The litter box should be kept in a consistent place that affords the animal some privacy.

Fortunately for most cat owners, kittens are innately house-trained before they are purchased, and do not need any specific training. Bladder and bowel control actually develops around the third week in a cat's life. When I am asked for advice by an owner whose cat has started eliminating in unusual places, the first thing I do is examine the cat for a physical or biological cause of the behaviour. An inflammation of the bladder or urethra is probably the most common cause. The burning sensation results in the cat urinating in the sink and on carpets and elsewhere. Similarly, blocked or painful anal sacs can cause a cat to urinate or defecate in strange places. And hormonal changes, physical injuries, chemical insults, illness and debility or surgery can all result in the unpleasant behaviour. But if all of these causes are eliminated, then the next step is to find out more about the cat's environment. Have the owners moved their home, or even just moved their furniture around? Have they redecorated? Have there been any new additions, humans or otherwise, to the family? Has there been a change in anyone's behaviour to the cat? Has the brand of cat litter been changed? Are there any stray cats hanging around outside? Questions like these must be asked because in the absence of a physical explanation and concomitent treatment, a behavioural reason must be found.

The first step in treatment is to determine, and if possible alter, the environmental cause of the problem. The second step is to counter condition the behaviour itself. This is one of the most difficult tasks of behaviour modification that one faces. The theory is this. The cat is restricted to a room in which it has not previously eliminated except in its litter box. It is provided with food and water and a clean litter tray filled with a type of litter that it has previous used. If the cat can be constantly watched, it can be allowed out of the room, but constantly watched means just that. If the cat starts to urinate or defecate in any area other than its litter tray, the second it does so it should be startled by something, like tossing a shoe next to it. The owner should remain quiet and unobtrusive when this is done. The idea is for the cat to associate the place and the act with the startling and unpleasant event, but not with the owner. I frequently use a hormone in tablet form for the cat, in conjunction with the behaviour modification approach.

Only 2% of the cases Roger Mugford sees are sex-related problems. I doubt that this genuinely reflects the incidence of sex-related problems, but rather indicates that owners look upon these problems as being trivial in comparison to aggression and destruction. I know one Great Dane who comes up on women from behind, lifts them up with his muzzle and carries them several feet forward. Crotching dogs are a nuisance to some, and an embarrassment to others, but owners seldom do more than apologetically mention the fact to their veterinarian.

In a similar vein, there is a Yorkshire terrier in Portman Square who developed a sexual obsession for a green plastic frog. He would snarl and growl at the owners if they tried to take it from him, would carry it off into the corner and do odious things with it. The owners would take it away while he was sleeping and put it on a shelf. The dog would search the apartment until he saw it, and would then sit for hours staring at it. Was it love, or simply lust?

Several years ago, Harrods sold stuffed toys that were perfect replicas of some breeds of dog; Yorkshire terriers, Old English Sheepdogs, and others. Little did they know that they were selling sex aids for canines.

Sexual mounting behaviour can begin in pups as early as six or seven weeks, although it usually begins at around twelve weeks of age. Mounting by both male and female pups is normal. It is part of the maturation process. If, however, it is a practice that, for one reason or another, rewards the dog, it can lead to behavioural abnormalities.

Roger Mugford has written an article on one such case, a Dachshund, whose sexual vigour with family and some visitors was so great that it was castrated at six months of age and subsequently treated by hormone therapy at eighteen months of age, but all to no avail. The children in the family, and the mother, were very attached to the dog, although she found his mounting behaviour repellent. Her husband wanted to get rid of the pet. Dr Mugford described the house as one of tense chaos, and saw similarities in the noisy way the children, through crying, and the dog, through barking, vied for the mother's attention. To use Dr Mugford's words: "Under most circumstances, the lady had a very effective dominant control of the dog. She reported, and I observed, that it followed her about the house with a glazed expression, in her words 'leering and flashing'. She explained that it did this because it knew it made her distressed."

"That analysis seemed to be correct in all except semantic detail: her practice was to shout at the dog when it made sexual advances and, if this did not deter it, she resorted to slapping and hysterical admonishment. The dog appeared to be very satisfied with this behavioural outcome; any contact with the lady owner was a patent reward."

"The dog had made a fairly sophisticated analysis of her behaviour. The dog would attempt to mount the children in and out of her presence, because either way their screams would attract the mother's attention. However, visitors were treated more selectively because they tended to adopt an embarrassed silence when 'propositioned' by the dog; they were only mounted in the mother's presence."

The conventional punishment that had been used on this Dachshund had only served to reinforce the unwanted behaviour, and so Dr Mugford used a more passive treatment and did the following. A leash was attached to the dog's collar and left trailing at all times, and the family were instructed to avoid touching or interacting with the dog if he showed any sexual activity. If he did, he was dragged by the leash into an unoccupied room and left there one to three minutes. If he barked while in the punishment room, the owners waited for thirty seconds before letting him out.

The owners had to do this eighty-four times on the first day of training. But after a week, his mounting activity was down to ten times a day, and after a month down to less than once a day.

My dog is now fifteen years old. As she has aged, her behaviour has changed. When she was younger, if children were visiting, she would lie down amongst them. Today, when children arrive, she retires to her basket. She retires to her basket because it is in the nature of Golden Retrievers to do so. Other breeds, as they grow older, become more irritable and snappy. Pet owners have to be prepared for the fact that their animal's behaviour will change with age. Most of us expect our pets to act "like they always have" all their lives and forget that one day they will be confronted with the same geriatric problems in their dogs and cats as they will have with their own parents.

Just as older people sometimes lose patience or forget things, old dogs and cats do as well. This means that behaviour that could be relied upon earlier in life may change and we have to be prepared to compensate for that. Honey is gutter-trained, and also trained to wander no farther than the end of the sidewalk, but always to stay on the sidewalk. This has meant that each summer I have been able to leave the front door of the clinic open and, after someone has watched her while she uses the gutter, leave her lying outside the front door. She would lie outside until she got too hot or thirsty, would wander in for a while, and then back outside to people-gaze. She has always been an ardent people-watcher. But last summer, when she was fourteen, she made a mistake. Instead of lying down on the sidewalk in front of the door, she lay down in the gutter. It could have been catastrophic, but fortunately, we saw her. She simply forgot what she was doing; an old age behavioural change. We, in turn, have had to change our approach with her and can no longer give her the freedom she previously enjoyed.

We have to make changes when we take her to the park as well. Given her freedom, she would still choose to do four lengths of dog paddle in the Serpentine, and half a dozen duck dives. But if she does, her old body is as stiff as a board the next day. Whereas, for all of her life we have let her exercise as much as she wants, now we have to change our ways and control it so that it is consistent each day.

Honey has a common old age problem in Golden Retrievers, and that is that she developed an arthritic change to the bones in her ears and as a result of that went deaf last year. This happens to many dogs, and its importance to her behaviour was that she could, of course, no longer respond to verbal commands. She had to be taught to respond to hand signals. Owners have to expect that their old dog's or cat's hearing and vision will deteriorate with age and adjust their care for the dog accordingly.

Finally, for unavoidable reasons, Honey has been on alternate day cortisone treatment for six months. Whereas, for her entire life, we could leave a barbecued steak on a plate on the floor and she would at most only lie beside it looking soulful, last month she raided the rubbish. That behavioural change should not be disciplined because it is a consequence of her medical treatment. Cortisone makes her hungrier and has changed her behaviour.

There are a few behavioural do's and don'ts that pet owners should apply to their older pets, and the most important is "let sleeping dogs lie". The old dog or cat should not be bothered or petted unless the pet actually solicits attention. Older pets should not have strenuous exercise, their diets should be watched and changed as the veterinarian suggests. Older pets should be treated with a little dignity, just as older people should, and we should be prepared to put up with a few quirky idiosyncracies in those last years. The pet that has been a good companion all its life has the right, as older people should, but are not necessarily granted, to a certain respect and consideration for its behaviour. Perhaps that is asking a lot. Western society still has to learn cultural respect for its oldest living generation of humans. To generalize this respect to all animals is perhaps asking for the impossible.

CHAPTER EIGHT

Pets in therapy

Claire was dying from cancer when she first went riding. Keith Webb, the founder of The Diamond Riding Centre for the Handicapped, told us about Claire at a meeting in 1981 of the Society for Companion Animal Studies. "A once active child," he said, "was reduced to lying on a sofa for most of the day. She rode once a week but her active mind also had to be occupied the rest of the time. So we set her to studying the care and management of ponies, their training and riding theory. Her essays and examination papers taught me more about horses than I had ever known before. Her practical tests were an ordeal for us, for to pass them on anything but merit would have been an insult to her intelligence. In the event of failure, there was no time to take the exams again as time was running out.

"Eventually, Claire was admitted to hospital for the last time. During her brief periods of consciousness the telephone would ring at the Centre and her favourite pony would set out for the ward. He would put his head through the open window for her to see him. The contrast between the clinical atmosphere of the ward and the shaggy, smelly pony was quite dramatic. When she died she was very happy. Her room was full of ponies; cards, pictures, models and ornaments. If there are any tears to shed, then they are for those of us who are left behind. We are the ones who have to come to terms with the harsh realities of our world."

Riding for the disabled is the best known and most broadly based use of animals in therapy for children and adults. There are over two hundred centres for riding for the handicapped in North America, and over one hundred and thirty in the United Kingdom alone. Riding for the mentally or physically disabled is a recognized form of animal therapy, but just about the only one.

That is not to say that domestic pets are not used in unique and exciting ways. The problem to date has been that almost all the reports on the therapeutic use of dogs and cats have been anecdotal and the medical profession and social sciences don't like anecdote; they like fact. Anecdote smacks of sentimentality, and as I have said before, sentiment is one of the last things that science wants to look at seriously.

Doreen Hutchinson, a Consultant Children's Psychiatrist in Stoke-on-Trent, uses her clients' attitude towards pets and their handling of them as guides to healthier behaviour. Her use of pets is based on family experience. "When the 1914–18 war ended," she says, "my father returned to the land fit for heroes to live in. After years as a prisoner of war with the Turks, building the railway through the Taurus mountains in conditions of gross deprivation and cruelty, he was in need of sensitive rehabilitation.

"He found it, not from a grateful government or an understanding community, but in a black Springer spaniel whom he called Tom."

It is certainly touching, but it may or may not be true. Science wants fact and controlled studies before embarking on the use of pets therapeutically. That type of scientific analysis is now emerging.

Animals have been used therapeutically for at least 200 years. In the eighteenth century The York Retreat, a mental hospice, used rabbits, poultry and other small animals to teach patients self control through having creatures weaker than themselves dependent on them.

More relevant to us, Dr J. H. S. Bossard, writing in 1944 in the journal, *Mental Hygiene*, said that pets serve as buffers or safety valves for human emotions, that they give the owner ego satisfaction and can act as a weather vane for the psychiatrist, telling him or her something about the owner. In the same year, the American Red Cross set up a rehabilitation programme for emotionally disabled airmen. Each patient was matched with a dog and participated in daily two hour dog training classes as part of his rehabilitation. This scheme at the American Air Force Convalescent Center in Pawling, New York, apparently showed positive results, yet there was no follow-up.

In fact, scientifically speaking, pet therapy stood still for twenty-five years, until Boris Levinson, of Yeshiva University in New York, published a book called *Pet Oriented Psychotherapy*.

Dr Levinson is the modern pioneer of pet therapy for individuals, and it all came about accidentally. It began one day when one of Levinson's clients, a withdrawn, distraught boy named Johnny, arrived early for his appointment. Jingles, Levinson's pet black Labrador, was still in the office as clients were not expected yet, and inadvertently Johnny and Jingles were left alone together. When Levinson returned to them, he observed that Johnny was at ease with the dog and, as it later transpired, this ease with the dog soon passed to ease with the dog's owner. Jingles had become the conduit for Levinson and the boy to make contact.

This serendipitous meeting subsequently brought Jingles a little fame in Levinson's dedication to his book.

> *This book is dedicated to Jingles, my co-therapist,*
> *To Whom I owe more than he owes me; . . .*
> *Who taught me more than I taught him;*
> *Who unveiled a new world of experience for me;*
> *Who doesn't care whether this book is dedicated to him or not;*
> *And Who will never learn about it.*

Levinson's hypothesis as to how pets can be therapeutic is quite simple. He regards interaction with pets as a half-way station on the road back to emotional well-being. He feels that contact with animate nature is important in the emotional development of the child. But it is important for the elderly as well. He says, "A pet can provide, in boundless measure, love and unqualified approval. Many elderly and lonely people have discovered that pets satisfy vital emotional needs. They find that they can hold on to the world of reality, of cares, of human toil and sacrifice, and of intense emotional relationships by caring for an animal. Their concepts of themselves as worthwhile persons can be restored, even enhanced, by the assurance that the pets they care for love them in return."

Levinson says that pets can help to off-set loneliness, make people more mobile, increase self esteem and confidence and increase contact with other people. Most important, they do not judge and offer criticism. This is why Johnny took to Jingles.

Boris Levinson is the theoretician of pet-facilitated therapy, but science, as I say, wants fact. Let me give you an example. Mrs Beatty, an old age pensioner client of mine, suffered from increasing hip-joint pain and eventually her physician recommended that she be given a new hip joint. Her dog, a spayed Cairn terrier with a tendency to being overweight, was kennelled while Mrs Beatty was in hospital for surgery, and remained in kennels for two weeks after Mrs Beatty returned home so that she could concentrate on her rehabilitation. Those two weeks were terrible for her. She was in too much discomfort to exercise and her use of the new joint was negligible. But for financial reasons, her dog could stay in kennels no longer.

When the dog was returned home, Mrs Beatty was distraught. She was instantly on the telephone to me. "She's nothing but a hairy balloon," she said. Many kennels will, if given the choice, return animals to their owner's in a plumper condition than when they went into kennels, if only to show "how happy" the dog was to be there. Samantha, the Cairn, had seen her opening and had gorged herself for three weeks.

Mrs Beatty was given some dietary advice for the dog and was told that Samantha's exercise should be increased. And so for Samantha, not for herself, Mrs Beatty started walking again. Now I know why she started walking again, and Mrs Beatty knows why she started walking again, but that is not enough fact on which to base a therapy. In the early seventies what was needed was a little more anecdote but also some proper scientifically controlled experiment. Boris Levinson had provided the theoretical basis. Sam Corson provided the scientific documentation.

Dr Corson is Professor of Psychiatry and Biophysics at Ohio State University. His wife, Elizabeth O'Leary Corson, is a Research Associate in the same department. Their work at the University involved studying chemical changes in the body associated with psychiatric disorders, and dogs were used in their studies. It so happened that the Corsons' laboratory and the dogs' kennels were one floor below the day room used by some of the emotionally disturbed people who were being counselled and treated at the hospital. One day one of these patients, a young teenager, heard the dogs barking and asked to visit them.

The request triggered a tangential thought for Corson, and applying the scientific thoroughness with which he approached his field of study, psychobiology, he decided to see if the use of pets in therapy would be of any value for patients who had failed to respond to the so-called "standard" forms of therapy such as drugs or electric shock. The Corsons set about matching the temperaments and personalities of dogs that they had at their disposal, such breeds as wire haired terriers, collies, beagles and cocker spaniels, to the needs of specific patients. In 1975, they published their initial results in *Current Psychiatric Therapies*, reporting exceedingly encouraging results. Psychotics who had previously been uncommunicative and bed-ridden, were transformed and eventually discharged from the hospital.

The Corsons' work gave factual scientific credence to Boris Levinson's theories and stimulated the scientific interest that was necessary if more was to be learned.

On a more personal note, Levinson's books and Corson's articles were answering questions I had been asking myself since graduating. Are small companion animals really of any value and concomitantly, are their veterinarians of any great or even mediocre social use? Until the last half century, the veterinarian's role was simple and obvious. It was to assist the agricultural industry to provide us with healthy animal protein as cheaply as possible. And, until the massed production of automobiles and tractors, to assist in the maintenance of our transport system. The needs were obvious and the role was precise.

But today most veterinarians work with companion animals. The role is obvious but many veterinarians question the need. One man who is a pioneer of good quality small animal veterinary medicine in the UK put it to me this way. "I feel myself akin to the hairdresser," he said. "I offer a service that makes people feel better but whose loss would not be an overwhelming burden."

In 1980, The British Small Animals Veterinary Association asked me to organise a symposium on Pets in Society. It was an ideal opportunity to find the best international authorities and the most recent scientific research and, quite selfishly, to answer the questions that were on my mind. With slight modification, "Pets in Society" became the first international symposium on "The Human–Companion Animal Bond".

Within weeks of our first letters going out to Europe and North America, I received a fascinating and long letter from a woman named Kathy Quinn. It was more anecdote, but this time from the patient.

It wasn't until a year later that I learned that Kathy Quinn had been placed in mental institutions thirty-six times in her life, and had spent a total of seven years living in fourteen different institutions, frequently in a straight jacket. She wrote, in part: "I've really known first hand about being lonely and isolated. . . . The professionals who have known me since I first came out of the institutions feel, along with me, it was my involvement with the animals that changed my life.

"I was once considered retarded – never to recover. In unique ways the dogs built my confidence, giving me a false sense of self-confidence by just their size and image of being aggressive dogs. I could walk down the street during the daylight hours without being afraid, but couldn't do it without the dogs."

Kathy Quinn continued to have problems with the police and with her German Shepherd, and finally a crisis occurred when she was threatened with the removal of her dog.

"I was told by a trainer that in order to save my dog, I would have to socialise it with people and in many different environments. Since I loved the dog, I forced myself to do just that without realizing that by socializing her, I was also being socialized. I learned to communicate with people this way, and by people wanting to know about my dog. The dog gave people a reason to come up to me when I would never go up to them.

"People will do a lot for their animals even though they might not take one positive step toward helping theirself knowingly.

"There have been several very shy – low self-esteem – no self-confidence people, like myself a while back, that had dogs that fit their personalities. The animals were not approachable just like all of us . . . . Since this time, I've done a lot of work on helping shy dogs become stable animals and what applies to treating the dogs can really work for people if applied properly."

Kathy Quinn is a top notch dog trainer today, as well as an animal photographer and magazine writer. She got in touch with me through Leo Bustad. Bustad, in addition, continued to collect anecdotal evidence of the therapeutic role of companion animals, and among others, recounted the story of a woman, Austrian by birth but living in the United States, who suffered from severe memory loss, suspected Alzheimer's Disease. She lived completely in the past and as the disease progressed she could no longer speak the English language. Other than a "yes" or "no", she never uttered anything in English. One day, a neighbour's dog, a Basset Hound named Audrey, came to visit and as she petted the dog, she said "Nice puppy, are you hungry"? Her daughter couldn't believe her ears. And subsequently, each time the dog visited it was spoken to in English, although she never resumed using the language with her family or with anyone else.

There is a wealth of anecdote such as this available today, but the most interesting study of the therapeutic value of pets for individuals comes from Michael McCulloch, a psychiatrist in Portland, Oregon.

As with the psychiatrist Levinson and the psychobiologist Corson, McCulloch's interest in the therapeutic use of animals was triggered by chance. A patient was referred to him for psychiatric evaluation because of depression. This 56-year-old married father of six suffered from kidney failure. He had received a kidney transplant from his son, but his body rejected it. Another transplant failed as well.

After compulsory medical retirement, he returned home

on dialysis and had one heart attack and repeated angina whenever he exerted himself. His wife had gone to work and he was at home alone during the day and was irritable, belligerent, argumentative and withdrawn from family, friends and his usual interests.

McCulloch says that his client reported feeling increasingly useless, angry at his physical restrictions, imprisoned by his dialysis machine and a burden to the rest of his family. Nestled among the information that McCulloch gleaned was the fact that the client had greatly enjoyed his childhood and adulthood pets; and McCulloch suggested that he get one. This in itself isn't surprising. Boris Levinson surveyed 435 members of the New York State Psychological Association in 1972 and discovered that over half had at one time or another recommended pets for home use in therapy.

McCulloch reports: "Considerable time was spent in finding the right animal as he wished to get another Basset pup. He became very much interested in contacting various dog breeders and finally going to pick out the dog. Within two weeks, his spirits were improved, his activity level was increased and with the arrival of the seven-week-old pup, the tension in the household markedly decreased. The antics of the animal caused laughter that had been conspicuously absent in the household for many months.

"The patient's spirits continued to improve. He was noticeably less angry and seemed very involved and interested in the training of the animal. The patient's communication with other family members took on a much more positive note, and he reported feeling much less preoccupied with his illness and was more willing to be physically active in walking and training the dog. He also stated that it was nice to be needed again. The patient continued to do well on his dialysis but suffered intermittent angina, and later another myocardial infarction. He survived that and has continued on home dialysis every other day. He has continued on a low dose of antidepressants, and he has remained absorbed in his pet dog, which he has named Hope".

McCulloch quite frankly had not foreseen that the improvement would be so dramatic, but where he differs from the other 51% of counsellors who have suggested using pets in therapy is that he wanted to know why the pet had been therapeutic and, once knowing why, whether he could generalise the experience and develop some criteria for using pets therapeutically for patients living at home and suffering from medical illness and depression. He drew the medical records of fifty patients whom he had seen in the last three years and who had histories of pet ownership. Thirty-one were available for the study. These people had suffered heart attacks, strokes, injuries resulting in permanent physical disabilities, endocrine disorders like complicated diabetes, severe gastro-intestinal problems, cancer and the like, all of which were permanently disabling and all of which resulted in a depression reaction.

McCulloch wanted to know three things; how these people felt their illnesses affected their lives, what they felt gave them a feeling of support during their illnesses and what influence they felt their pets had on them while they were ill.

The answers to the first part of his questionnaire corresponded with what was already known. These ill people felt they were a burden to others and that they could neither be physically active nor be able to enjoy their usual interests.

Their spouses, or close friendships were the most important supports they had. Returning to work was equally important. Most also felt that their pets improved their morale and were important sources of companionship. Only one of these people lived alone, and McCulloch says that by most standards the patients had social stability and adequate support systems. In spite of this, his patients felt that the presence of pets was an important addition towards coping with illness and depression.

In the third part of the questionnaire, the section concerning what influence they felt their pets had on them, twenty-nine out of thirty-one said that the "pet helped me to laugh and maintain a sense of humour." The same number said that the pet's affection was greatly appreciated, and twenty-six said that their pets helped them cope with isolation and loneliness. Over two-thirds of these patients said that their pets distracted them from worry, made them feel more secure, improved their morale and spirits, stimulated more physical activity and made them feel needed. Half of the patients said that at times they were too ill to care whether the pet was around, and a quarter of them worried about who would care for the pet if the illness got worse, or thought the pet was a nuisance. Four people felt that their pets were too much responsibility.

The most striking finding from this survey was how important these people felt their pets were to them during their illnesses. The life change caused by serious illness quite naturally increases the person's vulnerability, and with it the patient's reliance on support, even from a pet. Most of these people felt that they were burdens to their families; their self esteem was shattered. But having their pets depend on them for basic needs was one way in which they could cope with their own negative feelings about dependency.

With this information, McCulloch went on to make suggestions on how pets might be useful as aids in therapy. He emphasizes again and again that the use of pets does not displace other forms of therapy but rather augments or complements them. If a person has a "positive relationship" with a pet then the pet may be helpful if that person is plagued with:

1. Chronic illness or disability
2. Depression
3. Role reversal and negative dependency
4. Loneliness or isolation
5. Helplessness or hopelessness
6. Low self-esteem
7. Absence of humour

It is interesting to compare McCulloch's suggestions with the seven functions of pets that Aaron Katcher says could be expected to have some influence on physical health:

1. Something to decrease loneliness
2. Something to care for
3. Something to keep you busy
4. Something to touch and fondle
5. Something to watch
6. Something that makes you feel safe
7. Something to provide a stimulus for exercise

McCulloch urges caution in using pets in the home therapeutically. He lists five precautions:

1. Beware of increased vulnerability to the loss of a pet
2. Tailor the pet to the individual
3. Co-ordinate the use of pets with other therapy methods
4. Identify situations that are inappropriate for pets
5. Time the introduction of the pet into therapy so that contact with the pet can be fairly consistent.

As a psychiatrist, McCulloch sees the struggle to maintain self-esteem and dignity in the face of chronic debilitating disease as the biggest challenge. "For most it is hard to forget 'the way I used to be'. They mourn their loss of function and often set unrealistic expectations of their improvement only to be disappointed and lapse into despair. We must be prepared to help them use the lowest point of their disability as their new frame of reference. Then all progress will seem a relative success . . .. In an age of research when it is tempting to reduce emotions to biochemical reactions and to rely heavily on the technology of medicine, it is refreshing to find that a person's health and well-being may be improved by prescribing contact with other living things."

McCulloch's work, as well as Corson's and Levinson's, was in the use of pet dogs and cats in the home, but their results stimulated a new look at the use of trained animals in therapy.

Dogs have been trained in Europe, Britain and the United States for over fifty years to act as eyes for the blind. Their function is obvious; to be of physical assistance to the owner by guiding him or her when that person is outside the home. Now, the School of Social Work at the University of Pennsylvania wanted to look at the psychological and social significance of these dogs to their owners. Were they more than mere physical aids? A PhD thesis sponsored by the Guide Dogs for the Blind Association in Britain had previously explained how owners of guide dogs had high self-esteem and felt that they were the "elite" of the blind.

Alysia Zee, a social worker, designed two questionnaires,

sent to a number of people who had owned guide dogs for at least a year. The first questionnaire was designed to have the dog owner describe the nature of the relationship between the individual and the guide dog. She expected that the owners would describe their dependence on their dogs, but the results were intriguing.

These guide dog owners described a relationship of inter-dependence. Just as surely as the blind person needed the dog to act as a guide, so did the dog need the owner to regulate and reinforce its training, to reward work well done, to feed and to groom, to exercise and to talk and play with. The dogs needed affection and attention and protection from stress when upset by demands of work. I remember a colleague telling me of an incident in which he was involved when a guide dog was left with him for the day, to be anaesthetized and to have its ears syringed because of a particularly nasty and resistant infection. The dog recovered from its anaesthetic; the owner retrieved her and they left the surgery. Half an hour later, another client reported seeing the owner and the dog on a traffic island in the middle of a dual carriageway in the rush hour. The dog had guided her there, in quite the wrong direction, and then flatly refused to do anything more. The owner was distraught, not because of the personal risk to herself, but because she had selfishly demanded so much from her dog.

The needs and capabilities of blind individuals and their guide dogs in Miss Zee's survey were blended together as they were between the guide dog who had her ears syringed and her owner. They needed each other and this would quite naturally increase the owner's feeling of responsibility and self-esteem.

The second questionnaire enabled people to identify problems associated with blindness and asked what elements in their relationship with their guide dogs helped them or hindered them in dealing with these problems.

The problems that were identified as being most related to blindness include: frustration, over-protection by others, isolation, dependency, depression, sedentariness, fear of movement, rigidity of activities, self-consciousness and tension. I read that list to a client of mine who was recently given a guide dog, and he said it was uncanny; it was as succinct a resume of his feelings about his blindness as could be had. I asked him if he could describe any change in those feelings now that he had a guide dog, a Golden Retriever named Zephyr. He beamed and said that it was really beyond words. He had a new life. He loved everything about the dog, even its smell, which was the reason he had brought her in. (She had a skin infection.) Zee's owners reported that their dogs were catalysts for growth or change. The types of gains they referred to, and described, included an acceptance of life and stress, risk taking, expression of feelings, assertiveness, personal achievement, orientation to the present, relaxation, improved body image, faster walking pace, freedom of movement, security, self-control, self-awareness, separation from home, tolerance of various weather conditions and opportunities for social contact. In other words, these dogs are therapeutic in many more ways than just acting as eyes.

Work such as this has stimulated a fresh look at a therapy as successful as riding for the disabled. Just what is it that makes horseback riding therapeutic?

First of all, there is the obvious. The physically or mentally handicapped person is elevated physically, and for a change is looking down at others. That must be a psychological advantage. More important, those who live with or work with the disabled, rather than seeing the disability, for a change see the person's ability. The importance of touch is just as vital with the disabled as with others, if not more so, and the experience of sitting on and stroking a soft, warm animal is probably physiologically therapeutic. Joe Royds, a retired businessman who has been involved in riding for the disabled for over a decade, says of riding for mentally handicapped children that, "it seems to push a pipe cleaner up the blocked conduits of the mind". Some research out of New Mexico is a little more precise. It shows that mentally handicapped children who participated in therapeutic riding showed an increased ability to carry on conversation, and even greater syntax, than those who did not ride. Along with improved speech and physical dexterity, these children had greater self control. Perhaps the control of the horse led to greater control of self. Whatever the reason, riding and the greater exposure to the community that resulted from riding, had beneficial effects on the attitudes of the families as well as the riders. Children who viewed themselves as failures started thinking of themselves as people. The fascinating point of this to me is that, in a situation involving a severely mentally retarded child and a trained horse, we have an inversion of the whole process of socialization, for in these circumstances it can truly be said that the animal is domesticating the child.

Keith Webb has written as eloquently and pragmatically as anyone on the therapeutic value of riding for the disabled. He has described Ian, a spina bifida child, who gained coordination of his trunk muscles to walk, however clumsily, through riding therapy; and John, a withdrawn spastic child, rejected by his parents and in care of the Local Authority, who, through his riding, allowed people to help him to return to the world of reality.

Webb says, "We all need to feel a sense of pride in the achievement of those nearest and dearest to us. The opportunities open to the parents of a mentally handicapped child are few and far between. Many of our riders are given a Proficiency Certificate upon achieving some real goal. Unfortunately, Paul is so severely mentally handicapped that very little could be achieved, but he, too, received a Proficiency Certificate. It stated the truth – 'Paul has ridden for five years and loves his pony very much'. His mother broke down in tears for, she explained, no-one had ever taken any account of Paul, but now someone was prepared to declare to the world at large his ability to love."

A direct consequence of this recent research into the therapeutic role that pets can play is the Royal National Institute for the Deaf's Hearing Dogs for the Deaf Scheme. Dogs have been trained in the United States for almost a decade to act as ears for the deaf. In contradistinction to the type of outdoor work that guide dogs for the blind do, hearing dogs act in the home. They are on 24-hour alert for they must tell the owner that there is a knock on the door, or that the baby is crying, or that the kettle is whistling.

Deafness is one of the greatest sensory losses that we can suffer, and evokes the least sympathy. We simply lose patience with deaf people, and this further exacerbates their feelings of alienation, loneliness and frustration because of their disability.

Dogs are being trained as hearing dogs for two reasons. The first is obvious. A properly trained dog will act as ears for his or her owner. The second reason is less obvious but more therapeutic. Most people, 89% in the most recent survey, feel that their pet dogs understand their moods. Most of my clients feel the same, and indeed so do I. Whether the dog actually understand or not is academic. The important point is that we think that they do. My dog knows when I'm feeling happy and when I'm feeling sad. She knows when I need comfort. Now, translate that attitude to the deaf owner, a person who can't easily communicate his or her feelings because of the inability to carry on a verbal conversation. If the deaf owner feels that the pet dog understands his or her moods, then there is actual, although mute, communication. There is understanding and one little bit of the loneliness of deafness is lifted. This hypothesis will be tested scientifically once a sufficient number of hearing dogs have been placed in the UK.

What I have described so far is the therapeutic use of pets primarily in the home, but it is perhaps of lesser importance than pet therapy in institutions. A wide variety of small animals is being used in old folks homes, mental institutions, hospitals and prisons, and sometimes with startlingly therapeutic effect.

In order to understand how pets can be useful in institutions, it is best to describe first what these places are like. Professor Corson has described the social environment of geriatric institutions this way:

"Loneliness, depression, hopelessness, helplessness, boredom and low self-esteem are characteristics shared by many residents in custodial institutions, particularly in those catering to the aged. The social structure of a custodial institution tends to perpetuate and exacerbate the very deficiencies which brought the residents there in the first place. A vicious cycle of debilitation and social degradation and de-humanization is established."

The typical nursing home is a closed social group. It is usually mass-oriented and highly regimented, and because of that, leaves little room for the retention of a feeling of individual responsibility or a sense of dignity. People in old folks' homes frequently lose their sense of purpose, the feeling of being needed or respected, the feeling of being loved or being able to love. And on top of all of this, almost all nursing homes demand that their residents part with their pets when they are admitted. Many apartment houses and condominiums do the same, for that matter.

In 1975, due to lack of research funds, Professor Corson was forced to disband his dog colony at the Ohio State University Psychiatric Hospital. Serendipity, once more, intervened and led him to Donald De Hass, a dog owner and administrator of a large nursing home. De Hass was convinced of the benefits of animal companionship and had, indeed, always taken his well-tempered Doberman, Blue, on his rounds with him. Professor Corson's trained dogs were transferred to the nursing home.

The researchers developed a questionnaire that was incorporated into nurses' notes, including observations on the physical and emotional well-being of the resident, social activity with other residents and staff, changes in personal hygiene and appearance, changes in medication, etc. Videotapes were also made of the residents' interactions with the pet and with the staff.

The results, in many cases, were startlingly good. Jed, in his late seventies, had been a nursing home resident for twenty-six years. He was admitted after suffering brain damage in a fall, and was thought to be deaf and mute as a result of the accident. In the ensuing years, Jed was antisocial and apparently uncaring for those who cared for him. Jed's only form of communication was through grunts and mumbles. He spent most of his time sitting in silence, occasionally emitting outbursts of incoherent mumbling. Jed was one of the first residents to be introduced to a dog. Donald De Hass brought Whiskey, a German Shepherd/Husky cross, to visit him. Jed's reaction was immediate, and he spoke for the first time in twenty-six years. "You brought that dog," he said. Whiskey was the catalyst. He broke a communication barrier that Jed had erected twenty-six years before. Jed started to talk to the staff about the dog; about "his" dog. The nurses noted, and recorded, an improvement in Jed's disposition to the staff and to other residents.

Similar results were noted elsewhere. Some residents lived in cottages on the grounds, while others lived in dormitory-style buildings. Dogs helped to transform the cottage residents into a sort of extended family, while in the dormitories someone would voluntarily "adopt" the animal and take major responsibility for its care and feeding. The Corsons worried about possible cruelty to the animals, but this did not occur. They could not tell, however, whether the lack of cruelty was natural or due to close supervision by the nursing staff. One thing they did notice was that less retarded residents would often help more retarded patients to handle the pet carefully and gently.

In his research paper, Professor Corson concluded that "carefully selected, well-trained dogs offered the residents of a nursing home a form of non-threatening, reassuring,

Well-trained dogs . . . helped to break the cycle of loneliness, helplessness and social withdrawal

non-verbal communication and tactile comfort, and helped to break the cycle of loneliness, hopelessness and social withdrawal. Pet animals acted as effective socializing catalysts with other residents and staff and helped to improve the overall morale of the institution and create a community out of individuals, many of whom were separated, detached, unhappy and self-pitying . . .. In many cases the pet dogs involved the residents in walks and running bouts, helping to improve the physical and emotional status of the aged.''

There are today over four-and-a-half million Americans who are over eighty years of age, and by the end of this century that figure will be six million. And not only will there be more elderly, they will be older. This is a demographic shift which means greater effort, more resources and a bigger budget if we are to look after our oldest living generation. Professor Corson's work shows that, in a simple way, the life and dignity of some of these peope can easily be improved. And gratifyingly, some senior citizen homes are responding. Garwood Home in Illinois, for example, employs Molly, a four-year-old black retriever. Under the supervision of Queenie Mills, Professor Emeritus at the University of Illinois' Department of Human Development, Molly comes to work each day with the director of the nursing home, Arlene Keith. Molly was chosen because of her gentle nature, her responsiveness to humans, and her size. The Home wanted a large dog so that the residents would not trip over her. Professor Mills says, ''As people get older and they aren't so attractive any more, there isn't much touching or hugging. But it is so important. Molly doesn't make demands on anyone. She loves you in spite of how you feel or look.'' Ms Keith says, ''They love to watch her run. Many of the women congregate around the window when she runs outside and they comment on how beautiful she is. You can almost see them perk up as they watch, and when they leave there is more of a spring in their step.'' Garwood Home has experienced the same benefits from the presence of a dog as did Professor Corson's Castle Nursing Home. As at the facility that Professor Corson used, Garwood was the residence for a woman who had not spoken for two years, but when presented with a small puppy said her first word,

*"Many of the women congregate around the window
when she runs outside"*

"nice". More words followed and eventually she was communicating with people again.

As far as I am aware, Minnesota is the only state having a law that specifies that residents may bring their pets into state institutions. Although California has a law forbidding discrimination against elderly pet owners, permitting people over 60 to keep their dogs, cats, guinea pigs, hamsters, rabbits, fish, birds and lizards with them in government subsidized housing, and Connecticut and New York have similar laws in preparation, there is still a long way to go before pets in nursing homes are an accepted reality.

A more dramatic use of pets in institutions is their use in prisons. The Ohio State Hospital for the Criminally Insane has the oldest programme in existence in the United States. It all started eight years ago when one of the patients found an injured wild bird and tried to nurse it. David Lee, the resident psychologist, noticed that many of the men got involved with it, and got permission and some money from the superintendent to buy a fish tank and two budgies as an experiment. Interest spread through the hospital, but then one day one of the budgies disappeared. It was found in the duffel bag of a prisoner who was being transferred to serve out his time in a prison. He loved it and couldn't bear to leave it behind. Lee then decided that there might be benefits in the men having pets of their own, and having the responsibility of caring for them. Pets were not just randomly handed out to the patients, but rather these men had to earn the right to have them. Each person had to convince Lee that he was ready to take care of an animal.

Preparation involved the making of the animals' cages and hutches, and learning about their needs. Small animals, like guinea pigs and hamsters, and birds such as budgies and even cockatoos, were introduced, and the results were more far reaching than even David Lee had expected. The level of violence in the hospital wing in which animals were introduced – always high – dropped significantly. Prisoners made fewer suicide attempts, and their medication requirements decreased. Most important for Lee, trust and communication between the therapist and the prisoners increased.

Violence in the other wards increased, however. They

wanted pets as well. But then a startling thing happened. The prisoners with pets decided they would help their fellow prisoners by breeding from their pets. They repaired the abandoned greenhouse in the prison grounds and became market gardeners. With the money they raised from the vegetables they grew, they bought breeding stock and bedding material and were soon able to supply the rest of the hospital. Today, they even supply the town pet shop with young pets.

I remember seeing a short film made in the prison in 1979. Michael McCulloch, the psychiatrist who brought the film over to Scotland for us to see, gave a running commentary on the prisoners who were seen with their animals in the film. One of them spoke to the cameraman, with a blue budgie perched on his shoulder. Every few words he would turn and kiss the budgie, and the budgie would gently peck him. "This is my first friend," he said. "I love him and he loves me. I didn't know what love was until I was given this bird." McCulloch explained that this man was, in fact, a multiple murderer.

Since the initial introduction of small animals on to the

*Preparation involved the
making of the animals' cages and hutches*

wards, the pet therapy programme at Lima State Hospital has continued, and today they have, among other pets, rabbits, deer and geese. One deer came from a zoo where vandals had stoned it. The prisoners nursed it back to health. So far there have been no instances of animal abuse at the prison, and David Lee doesn't expect any. He thinks that no-one would dare harm a pet for fear of retribution from the other patients. I hate to think of what the prisoners would do to the zoo vandals.

The most recent, most complete and most scientific study on the therapeutic use of pets in institutions was published in 1982 by Ingrid and Peter Salmon, two Consultant Psychologists in Melbourne, Australia.

The Salmons knew of the Corsons' work with pet-facilitated therapy on psychiatric patients who had failed to respond to traditional therapies such as psychotherapy, drugs, electric shock and occupational and recreational therapy. And a more local doctoral thesis had told them how pets can provide consolation, reduce stress and assist in coping with traumatic events during adolescence. They were aware of the work at the Castle Nursing Home where dependent, infantile and self-neglecting patients became more responsible and self-reliant after pets were introduced into the Home.

In 1981, using the Caulfield Hospital in Melbourne, they began a study, the objective of which was to determine whether or not a pet in a hospital had a quantifiable therapeutic effect upon the patients' health and well-being. Sixty patients, in two wards, whose average age was eighty were actively involved in the study, while similar patients in a third ward acted as the controls. Honey, a Labrador trained by the local Guide Dogs Association, was the pet that they introduced.

The Salmons were very thorough in their preparation and involved the nursing staff, the occupational therapists and themselves in monitoring the events that followed. In the first week, Honey wouldn't settle down. She was boisterous and restless and kept leaving the hospital whenever a door was left open. Although some patients enjoyed her presence, others were not at all enthusiastic and some of the staff objected to all the attention that was being focused on her. In her fifth week at the hospital, Honey got lost, but her loss had a catalytic effect on everyone. The uninterested patients and the dissenting staff joined the enthusiasts in their concern for her safety. When she safely returned and settled down, it was as if a family member had returned.

The Salmons questioned both the patients and the staff before Honey was introduced, and six months later, asking them what benefits or problems Honey would, or did, bring to the wards. The staff and patients both anticipated the same benefits; that she would provide company, friendship, enjoyment, something to talk about and love and affection. Eighty per cent of the patients and staff felt that she would do these things, as well as make the ward happier and more like home. At the end of the first six months 90% of the staff and patients felt that she had actually done these things.

Between 10% and 20% of the patients had worried about possible barking, smell, mess, discipline or that the dog would simply get in the way, but at the end of six months virtually none of them experienced any worries about Honey. On the other hand, half of the staff had anticipated detrimental effects. Over a third of them had been worried about her training and discipline, about Honey getting in the way, about her barking or her smell or the mess she would make. One quarter of the staff had worried about the increased workload they would have, and about the grooming she would need, complaints they would receive, frights that Honey would give to people, and possible cruelty she would suffer. But after six months, all of these worries had disappeared completely, with the exception of two. Twenty per cent of the staff still experienced problems with discipline with Honey, and with her getting in the way.

The occupational therapist thought that Honey was terrific. She said, "She is a wonderful participant in my movement to music group!" So did the staff. The report from Ward 10 said "The ward has an atmosphere now with the dog being there. Everyone knows her and those who can communicate make it very obvious that she is needed. She has made life very interesting for the staff and has made some of us very happy." The Ward 11 report said "The ward is more like a home now. Most of the ladies just like to see her around . . .. The response from visitors has been very positive."

After six months, when the Salmons compared the group of people who had exposure to Honey and the group that did not, they observed that the Honey Group "were more easy-going, less withdrawn and more interested in others. They slept fewer hours, spent less time in bed and less time alone."

They observed that patients were significantly happier, that they laughed and smiled more often and that their desire to live increased. They were more responsive and interested in others and their relationships with each other, and with the staff, improved. At the beginning of the programme, the average patient spent sixteen hours alone each day. By the end of the first six months this had been reduced to eleven hours.

All of this happened simply and inexpensively, through the introduction of a slightly extrovert Labrador on to a hospital ward. There were no worries about disease. Honey was under the supervision of a veterinarian from the Veterinary School at the University of Melbourne, and the hospital administration knew that disease problems that might occur through the introduction of a dog on to the ward were no greater, and probably less, than through the introduction of a new patient.

But what effect did this have on Honey? Well, she got fat! Initially, over one third of the staff worried about the demands that would be placed on Honey, the number of masters she would have, and the attention she would get, but none of these things proved to be a problem. Her only problem stemmed from the chocolates and biscuits with which she was bribed by some patients. There was some jealousy amongst some patients, who vied for her attention, but the psychologists thought that at least it broke the non-responsiveness that was there before.

Michael McCulloch has said that pets should not be looked upon as a panacea for all sorts of emotional or physical illnesses, but there is now enough scientific evidence to show that, through proper use, pets can act as catalysts in re-socializing people who have been placed in institutions. The pet can be the ice-breaker leading to other therapies, or simply strengthen the patient's ego, by responding honestly and with no strings attached to the patient's needs. Pet therapy, however, will not succeed if it is introduced carelessly. One mid-western American nursing home introduced some gerbils to their patients. Leo Bustad says the gerbils "got stomped on" by the patients. These people were farmers and gerbils, to them, were too much like rats.

Any pet therapy programme must begin by having its objectives defined and then by having the commitment of the staff. Jim Hutton, a social worker in Hertfordshire, has both of these, and uses animals when he sees fit. He has described how he has used ferret handling with two anti-social teenage boys, to gain their trust and to help them learn about themselves. He says "We began to discuss kindness, concern, encouragement and rewards. We contrasted this with an authoritarian approach to the (ferrets) and pondered on the possible consequences. The analogy was inevitably drawn between some of their own behaviour and that of the ferrets; if handled correctly, they respond with loyalty and friendship, but if handled incorrectly . . . they BITE!"

Pet therapy programmes need professional supervision. Playing alone with a pet may reinforce the very problem one wants to overcome in a withdrawn child, for example. The type of animal, its age or sex (or lack thereof); all of these facts must be considered. All the staff must be involved, including, of course, the cleaners or janitors, and proper veterinary support should be available from the very beginning. The objectives of the programme should be defined before anything is done. From what we already know, in a properly supervised manner a dog or a cat, or even a bird, can make people feel more secure and less lonely. It can give companionship and encourage activity. Most important, in an institution or home where many people have lost the ability to do so, it can make them do something that nothing else can – it can simply make them smile.

Epilogue

Just before I began writing this book my own dog, Honey, was worryingly ill. I wondered whether she would survive for very long but she responded magnificently to her treatment.

I started writing in the late autumn. I took time off work one day each week and, with Honey in the back of the camper, and with the heater left on in it all day, I would park her outside the Westminster Library while I got myself organized inside. I took her with me each week because I figured that at her age and in her condition she was entitled to a few extra pleasures. Sleeping in the back of the camper is one of the best.

At Christmas we left Honey in London while we visited my parents in Florida, and I wrote the first half of this at the Sarasota Library. Honey's surrogate was a geriatric Bassett Hound who, each afternoon, went for what seemed to be a clockwork controlled slow, and I mean *slow*, walk past our house. She was accompanied by an equally slow, but much younger, cat. They made a scene as if from Disney, the old fogey and her nurse. They were rib-crackingly funny, they looked so absurd.

Right now I'm in the Lenox Library in the Berkshires. My family is here in Massachusetts for three weeks. Honey's surrogates are Gomer the goat, Julius the rooster, a rabbit, a dog, a cat, two horses and a pony, all of whom live next door to where we are staying. Stacey, a corpulent black and white thing, ambles up each time I barbeque supper, hoping for some fuel for her corpulence. My parents have driven down

The old fogey and her nurse

from Ontario and have brought their weird new dog, Bejo, with them. My mother says that Bejo barks when she is happy. She is happy all the time. My kids have begged that Bejo stay with us for the three weeks. They didn't beg quite so ardently that their grandparents stay as long.

Each evening we put food out for a racoon that visited on the night we arrived. Other than his crashing into the barbeque on subsequent evenings, we have only seen him once since that first visit. Tamara, my youngest daughter, keeps a scorecard on who has seen how many deer. She has seen six so far and is the leading contender for the deer stalking prize.

It doesn't seem to matter whether we are in urban or suburban, or even the most rural of settings, my family seems to be surrounded by animals. When I was a boy we had dogs, cats, birds, fish and reptiles. Living in Toronto, we had even more. For years we had racoons living in the garage of our house, and would trace their comings and goings by the footprints they left as they used the roof of the parked car as a springboard up into the wooden rafters of the building. Wildlife is still a part of life in Toronto. Racoons and foxes use the ravines to move right into the heart of the city.

Professor Ingemar Norling tells me that there are now plans in Sweden for integrating their wildlife into their urban environments. The animals have done it themselves in Canada, although most people don't like their presence. Rabies is the reason.

As a veterinarian, however, I almost always see dogs, cats and birds, and I see them, and they are brought to me, as members of the family. They are family members because we feed and protect them. We take them to the veterinarian the way we take our children to the paediatrician. More than half of us share our bedrooms with them, and probably half of those people actually share their beds with their pets. We feel a kinship with them and buy them birthday gifts, take family photographs that include our pets, and grieve over them when they die, as we grieve when a friend or relative dies. We think of our pets as friends, or confidants, because we confide in them and think that they understand our emotions and feelings.

We do these things because pets satisfy some of our basic needs. Most important, a pet satisfies our need to nurture. Through talking to them, touching them or just looking at them, we fulfil our instinctive need for attachment. They also make us laugh, or just smile. We selectively breed them for these purposes. We breed them to be easy to carry, or for extra soft coats. We breed them to have large eyes and flat foreheads. We breed them to be bright and sparky and to keep youthful qualities throughout their lives. We breed them to look graceful, or just odd for that matter. But however we breed them, in our minds they retain innocence for life. They have the innocent quality of children forever. Children grow up, but the pet remains the same. It is always reliable, immutable to change, and because of this it provides us with a constancy in our lives. Orwell's *1984* and Toffler's *Future Shock* may come true, but a dog is a dog is a dog.

When we grieve when a pet dies, the grief can be devastating. It can be similar to the grief that we feel when a relative or close friend dies. It can be worse, in its own way, because many of us feel we are silly or self-indulgent when we feel such sadness, and we don't allow ourselves to grieve as we really need to.

. . . family photographs that include our pets . . .

In all of these ways we actually incorporate our pets into the human social system. We give them human privileges. But there is a dark side as well. The majority of dogs and cats in Britain and North America will, at some time in their lives, have their privileges arbitrarily withdrawn. They will be left on roads or city streets, or will be taken to animal shelters to be killed.

Dogs and cats are not simply products of nature. They are

also products of culture. As our culture has changed, the role we want our pets to play has also changed. We have changed their forms, personalities and capabilities as our cultural needs dictated. With the increasing urbanization of Western society, and the shearing of people from their roots, pets have taken on an increasing role in companionship. I only see selected pets, the pets of people who feel the desire or responsibility to care for them as best they can. These people are usually strongly attached to their pets, and the pets offer them many things in return. They can have a beneficial physiological effects on their owners, actually lowering their blood pressure. Statistically, you have a greater chance of being alive one year after having a major heart attack if you have a pet than if you don't. They can act as ice-breakers and help you meet people, and can be therapeutic, giving something to do, offering unconditional affection and raising your self-esteem. They can also cause emotional problems that would not arise if they were not there. Doreen Hutchinson, a Consultant Children's Psychiatrist, has recounted this story of one dog that did all of these things.

A family doctor asked Dr Hutchinson to see Louise, a

We breed them to look graceful, or just odd . . .

four-year-old child suffering from a bereavement depression after the death of her elderly Labrador, Dan. Louise's family was closely bonded and very attractive, and it quickly became evident that the parents were grieving for the dog too.

Louise's mother had been married for six years before she became pregnant, but as soon as she was, she felt surprisingly ill and needed her husband's comfort and support. But when she was four months into her pregnancy, he left her for another woman.

Louise's mother was devastated. She felt lonely, isolated and terribly depressed. Her only companion was Dan, the Labrador. He slept in her bedroom, on a rug by her bed, made himself available for tickles and hugs and strokes even in the early hours of the morning when she could not sleep, and forced her out of the house twice a day to exercise him. Louise's mother thought of suicide, but Dan's presence and needs helped her to overcome the feeling. In retrospect she felt that Dan looked after her better in the last half of her pregnancy than her husband had in the first half.

After Louise was born, her mother felt so weak physically that she was unable to take Dan for his exercise. Dan, of course, didn't know that. All he knew was that he wasn't being taken, so he took to sitting at the garden gate in hopeful anticipation.

One day a regular passer by called at the house to ask if there was a reason why the dog was at the gate each time he passed. On being told why, he asked Louise's mother if she would permit him to take Dan out for his evening exercise. She agreed, and both the man and the dog seemed to enjoy the event. It became a regular exercise.

In the beginning, the man used to drop Dan off at the gate, but later he was invited in for tea, and soon he started doing some odd jobs around the house.

The man married Louise's mother soon after her divorce came through. Dr Hutchinson says that Louise loves her new father and feels a rapport with him, as Dan did. She says that Louise's mother and her new husband might never have met, were it not for Dan. They are both shy and reserved people. When Dan died they felt that they had lost one of the deepest friendships possible. They had.

Dr Hutchinson's part was easy, she says. She helped the family transmute their grief at Dan's loss into gratitude that they had known him. And as the parents coped better with the loss, so did Louise.

It doesn't matter why Dan took to sleeping in Louise's mothers' bedroom. The important fact is that Louise's mother thought he did it to protect her. It doesn't matter why he really made himself available for a little hug and tickle in the middle of the night. What is important is that it gave Louise's mother comfort. It doesn't matter why Dan willingly went off for some exercise with a stranger. It is only important that Louise's mother felt that if Dan could trust a man, then perhaps she could. It doesn't matter that their grief at this death was for his symbolic role. My grief when Honey dies will be the same. The importance is that it is real grief at a heartfelt loss, and should be respected. It doesn't matter that Dan, the Labrador, is a creation of Western culture; that in another culture he might simply be eaten. What does matter is that the family felt a kinship with him, that they thought of him as a product of nature, innocent and untainted by human vices.

Most of the animals I treat have stories to tell, sometimes as dramatic as Dan's. The stories can be innocent or dark. The pet can symbolically, or in reality, represent something of importance to its owner, be it an incident or a mood. The pets I see, the cared for pets, all represent something. I seldom hear these stories, nor indeed should I. When I do, it is usually in that brief period after the death of a pet, when the emotional barriers are transiently lowered.

When I began practicing veterinary medicine, the satisfaction of work came from knowing that sometimes I could make an animal's life more enjoyable. I still have that pleasure, but it has been good to learn that sometimes I can do the same for its owners. Occasionally, I draw back and think "this is a soap opera!" If I'm a little tired and worrying about the medical side of a case, I might like the owner to simply get lost and stop bawling about how important Mitzy is to her, and just let me concentrate on getting her better. But Mitzy *is* important to her, and my nurses and I are among the few people in whom Mitzy's owner can emotionally confide. Mitzy's owner might exasperate me. Sometimes I might feel that she is plain nuts. It can be difficult not to use your own set of values on other people and wonder why they can't cope with what you consider to be a surmountable problem, especially when the problem is owner-made. It is even more difficult when the problem becomes coloured with the cloying, saccharin sweetness of sentiment that surrounds and symbolizes the relationship that many people have with their pets.

Almost all the stories I hear are sentimental ones. James Thurber, never one to get mired in syrup, wrote that "Man is troubled by what might be called the Dog Wish, a strange and involved compulsion to be as happy and carefree as a dog, and I hope that some worthy psychiatrist will do a monograph on it one of these days."

Thurber would be happy today, with psychiatrists like Aaron Katcher and Michael McCulloch fulfilling his hopes. I'm happy too that they are taking these sentimental stories seriously, and are writing about the meanings and the values of our relationship with other animals. I'm happy to know that half of my clients are not nuts! I'm happy to know that I'm not nuts. I'm happy to know that my dream of retiring to the countryside and looking out of the breakfast-room window onto a field of happily grazing Golden Retrievers will not result in my licence to practice being withdrawn. In my happiest dream, as I sit eating my blueberry muffins, smelling the coffee brewing, I look out at them and they, all in unison, lift their heads, look in at me and smile, as Golden Retrievers do, and wink, knowingly.

FURTHER READING

There are few books on the subject of the relationships that people have with their pets. Most of the work that is reported here has been published in scientific journals, and the Newsletter of the Group for the Study of the Human–Companion Animal Bond has been my major source.

International symposia on "The Human – Companion Animal Bond" have been held in Dundee, Scotland in 1979, in London, England in 1980 and in Philadelphia, Pennsylvania in 1981. Additional meetings on the same topic have also been held during this time in Nottingham and Cambridge, England and in Paris, France. I have drawn liberally from papers presented at these meetings. I have also used publications from The Joint Advisory Committee on Pets in Society – Australia.

The following books have been used.

Pets and Human Development. Boris Levinson PhD, Charles C Thomas, Springfield, Illinois, 1972

Pet Oriented Child Psychotherapy. Boris Levinson PhD, Charles C Thomas, Springfield, Illinois, 1969

Interrelations Between People and Pets. Bruce Fogle DVM, MRCVS, Ed. Charles C Thomas, Springfield, Illinois, 1981.

Anatomy of an Illness as perceived by the patient. Norman Cousins. W. W. Norton & Co, New York, 1979

Man Meets Dog. Konrad Lorenz, Methuen & Co, London, 1954

Understanding Your Dog. Michael Fox, Blond & Briggs Ltd, London, 1974

Behaviour, Development and Training of the Cat. Frederic J Sautter and John A Glover, Arco Publishing Co Inc New York, 1978

Animals, Aging and the Aged. Leo K Bustad, University of Minnesota Press, Minneapolis, Minnesota, 1980

Pet Animals and Society. R S Anderson Ed. Balliere Tindall, London, 1975